D0892547

OFFICIAL WTF TAEKWONDO

ABOUT THE AUTHOR

David Mitchell began studying the martial arts whilst at the University College of Cardiff. Previous to that, his experience in fighting arts was limited to rugby! He started with judo and represented his university at a number of inter-college matches. When karate began to spread throughout Britain during 1964, he opened the first karate club in Wales and went on to become the secretary of the Welsh Karate Board. He also studied taekwondo and was involved with the pioneers of that art when they set up Welsh taekwondo during 1966. Since then, he has worked closely with the present taekwondo governing bodies and has travelled to Korea, the home of that art. Whilst there, he studied the development and practice of WTF taekwondo.

In 1977, the author was appointed to the Martial Arts Commission, an umbrella body for all of the martial arts. He is the general secretary of the Commission and, in addition, is treasurer of the European Karate Union and the World Union of Karatedo Organisations.

He is an expert on combat sport competition theory and has collaborated to produce all manner of technical bulletins and information now adopted by the world and European bodies. His international connections have allowed him to research taekwondo directly, instead of through indirect sources. Accordingly, he is the ideal person to write this book.

Also published by Stanley Paul

QIGONG – CHINESE MOVEMENT AND
  MEDITATION FOR HEALTH
Danny Connor with Michael Tse

TAI CHI
Danny Connor

WING CHUN
Yip Chun with Danny Connor

THE JUDO MANUAL
G Hobbs and T Reay

OFFICIAL WTF TAEKWONDO

David Mitchell

The Martial Arts Commission of Great Britain

Stanley Paul
London

Stanley Paul and Co Ltd

An imprint of Random House (UK) Ltd
20 Vauxhall Bridge Road, London SW1V 2SA

Random House Australia (Pty) Ltd
20 Alfred Street, Milsons Point, Sydney 2061

Random House New Zealand Ltd
18 Poland Road, Glenfield, Auckland 10

Random House South Africa (Pty) Ltd
PO Box 337, Bergvlei 2012, South Africa

First published 1986
Reprinted 1987, 1989, 1990, 1992, 1993, 1994

Copyright Text and Illustrations © Antler Books Ltd 1986

The right of David Mitchell to be identified as the author of
this work has been asserted in accordance with the Copyright,
Designs and Patents Act, 1988

Set in Linotron Sabon
by Input Typesetting Ltd, London

Printed in England by Clays Ltd, St Ives plc

A catalogue record for this book is available upon request
from the British Library

ISBN 0 09 163441 5

Photography by Mike O'Neill
Line drawings by MJL Cartographics

CONTENTS

1. The Origins of Taekwondo   6
2. Practising Taekwondo   10
3. Developing Force in Taekwondo Techniques 16
4. The Stances of Taekwondo   23
5. The Weapons of Taekwondo   30
6. Basic Techniques of Taekwondo   40
7. Taekwondo Blocking Techniques   58
8. Taekwondo Combination Techniques   70
9. Taekwondo Patterns   81
10. Pre-arranged Sparring in Taekwondo   86
11. Free Sparring in Taekwondo   98
12. Competition Taekwondo   108
13. Taekwondo Destruction Techniques   114
14. Fitness for Taekwondo   121
15. Safety in Taekwondo Training   137
16. Glossary of Terms used in Taekwondo   144
Basic Taegeuks for Practice   164
Acknowledgements   180
Index   181

CHAPTER 1:
THE ORIGINS
OF TAEKWONDO

Man: Survivor to Warrior

The name taekwondo means simply 'way of the foot and fist'. Although this name was first introduced in 1955, the martial art which it describes has its origins back in mankind's primitive past.

The earliest of man's recognizable ancestors were not equipped with sharp claws or fangs. They were not exactly fleet of foot and had no special adaptations such as the ability to fly away from danger. Yet they found themselves amid carnivores and wild animals capable of preying easily upon them. They did, however, have something the other animals did not and that was a relatively advanced brain. This allowed them to develop survival aides such as weapons. At first these were whatever came to hand – stones, branches of trees, bones of large animals and so forth. Later, as knowledge in working wood and flint accumulated, the weapons became custom-made and more effective.

The possession of weapons allowed mankind to change its pattern of living from the retiring scavenger and plant-eater to predator. The males of family groups hunted together and developed primitive tactics which allowed them to kill large and aggressive animals. The successful families bred and multiplied until contact between them became commonplace and the first communities appeared, sharing resources and burdens between the members. Competition for these same resources would inevitably have led to clashes between groups of hunters when, for the first time, hunting tactics could be applied to other human beings.

The hunter bands eventually became armies of warriors led by the most successful fighters, making common cause against competing communities. The horse, once domesticated, provided a means of rapid deployment where whole corps of warriors could arrive swiftly at a military objective, attack it and move on to others. Projectile weapons developed into longbows and spears, the former providing a stand-off weapon capable of killing from a distance and the latter arming large numbers of foot soldiers in their support role for the cavalry.

The need for capturing but not killing marauders necessitated non-lethal forms of combat. Man's first unarmed combat would have been inherited from his ape ancestors – tussling, scratching, flailing and biting – but this too would have developed to keep pace with the increasingly sophisticated warfare of a hunter/ warrior community. Nevertheless, such combat would not have the same importance as armed warfare, since one trained man with a weapon is worth several unarmed men. For this reason unarmed combat by the military caste would not be developed to as high a degree as the weapon arts.

Those members of the community denied access to military training or weapons would be thrown back on their own resources if they wished to defend themselves from marauders. These resources would include a category of weapons adapted from everyday items such as the walking stick and the staff. They would also have included a system of unarmed combat to be used when no weapon was to hand. In many ways, the systems developed by the non-military castes were more advanced and their contribution to the present-day practice of taekwondo cannot be ignored.

The Martial Arts of Korea

The earliest indications of warfare in the Korean peninsula can be seen in the wall paintings of the Kokuryo Dynasty. This covered the period AD 37 to 668. Some of the tombs excavated in the vicinity of the Apro River depict what seems to be unarmed combat between men dressed in loincloths. The most detailed of these are to be found in the Kakjeochong, Samsilchong and Muyongchong burial chambers. Apart from these enigmatic paintings, there is no other record of systematized martial art practice at that time.

At the beginning of the Silla Dynasty, the kingdom was restricted to southeast Korea but through the actions of its young warrior caste – the *Hwa rang* – its influence spread throughout the whole peninsula. The Hwa rang were experts at archery, swordfighting, horseriding and unarmed combat. Between the months of July and August, an annual national festival was held at which the Hwa rang demonstrated their skills. Silla overran the southwestern Korean kingdom of Baekje with the help of Chinese forces and brought to an end 642 years of independence. The entire population and not just the armed forces of Baekje were well schooled in the martial arts and these were assimilated into the Hwa rang's martial art syllabus.

In the Koryo Dynasty (AD 953 – 1392) founded by Wang Kyon, this interest in martial arts was systematized and taught to the Korean military forces under the name soo bahk. One of the most famous exponents of *soo bahk* was the military commander-in-chief to the sixteenth King, Ui Jong. An annual unarmed combat tournament was held during May and participation by soldiers was compulsory. The winner was given an important government post and three eventually became generals of the armed forces. The Yi Dynasty extended for the period AD 1392 – 1907 and, during it, two notable training manuals on martial arts' technique were published. These were the thirty-second volume of the Korean History Book and the Military Arts Manual. The latter described twenty-four techniques.

The Development of Taekwondo
During the Japanese occupation of Korea (1907–1945), practice of the native Korean martial arts was at first suppressed but later, when Koreans were inducted into the armed forces on the side of Japan, their practice was once more allowed to increase the fighting ardour of the otherwise unwilling population. During the period of occupation, the Japanese fighting arts of karate, kendo, aikido and judo were introduced to the Korean armed forces with the result that many techniques were adapted and incorporated within existing Korean systems. In some cases, whole styles of Japanese martial arts were adopted with minor changes to bring them into line with Korean practices. The Koreans have always been interested in high kicks and destruction techniques and introduced these techniques into the Japanese systems.

At the end of the Second World War, there were five major martial arts academies in Korea. These were the Mooduk Kwan, the Jido Kwan, the Changmu Kwan, the Chungdo Kwan and the Songmu Kwan. Within the academies were twelve styles of martial art. A division occurred at this point between those who wished to preserve the martial art character of their schools and those who were interested in developing a combat sport. The first championships were held in 1956 and, soon after, an umbrella body known as the Korean Taesoodo Association was set up. The first president of the Association was Choy Myong-shin and, in 1964, the Korean Taesoodo Association joined the Korean Athletic Association and became government-recognized.

In 1965, the body changed its named to the Korean Taekwondo Association at the recommendation of General Choi Hong Hi. Choi founded the *chang hun* style of taekwondo which is based upon his early knowledge of soo bahk and taekyun, plus techniques adapted from Japanese karate. The presidents of the Korean Taekwondo Federation since its inception were Choy Myong-shin, Choi Hong Hi, No Byong Jik, Kim Yung Chi and Kim Un Yong.

From 1959, taesoodo/taekwondo began a programme of international development. In 1972 the Korean Taek-

wondo Association founded the World Taekwondo
Federation and based it at the Kukkiwon in Seoul. The
first world championships of taekwondo was held there
in May 1973. As a result of the WTF's energy and
enthusiasm, taekwondo is now listed as an Olympic
sport. It is also the national sport of Korea and is taught
to all members of the Korean armed forces. It has been
used in hand-to-hand fighting with great success.

What is Taekwondo?
Taekwondo is what is termed a 'hard', or 'external',
style of martial art. This adjective is used to describe
the muscular force used in the development of its techniques and it is therefore quite dissimilar from the softer
Korean martial arts such as hapkido. These respond to
rather than originate attacks and use the opponent's
strength against him. Taekwondo is, however, more
than just a collection of military techniques; it is also a
form of mental training.

A taekwondo kicking
technique

CHAPTER 2: PRACTISING TAEKWONDO

The practice of taekwondo involves techniques which by their nature are potentially hazardous both to the third party and to oneself. For this reason, training must involve physical and mental discipline. Taekwondo is so much more than a mere fighting system. Its practice is intended to have a beneficial effect upon the student's character and therefore his attitude is one of the most importance factors in whether training will be successful or not. The serious student who listens to what he is told, practises that which he is shown and who respects his colleagues and the class teacher will progress further.

The Correct Attitude
This attitude is more than just a vehicle for learning technique; it is a character-forming exercise in its own right. Through self-discipline and respect, the student develops a sensitivity for the needs of others and a modest pride in his achievements. The good taekwondo student will exhibit politeness in his dealings with other students and the teacher. He will avoid comparing his own achievements with those of his colleagues since this can lead to negative pride in some directions and envy in others. The responsibility of the teacher to the students is great. The teacher represents the embodiment of taekwondo's ideals and it is therefore imperative that an even more rigorous grading system is employed to select him.

If the teacher takes no care of his personal appearance and directs the class wearing a filthy training tunic, his students will assume that there is no taekwondo virtue in pride of appearance and respect for the practice of the art itself. If he knocks the students around during free sparring, his students may imagine that bullying tactics are the norm and inflict them on other grades.

For the newcomer to taekwondo, there is a long and arduous path to the black belt. This is based upon a training syllabus which introduces new techniques at regular intervals, so the student is constantly learning a series of more difficult techniques. The beginner contends with a short selection of the very basic moves and practises these over a period of three months or so. At the end of that time he is assessed by means of a grading examination to see whether his standards have reached a specified level. If they have, his level of competence is defined by a coloured belt. The student must never ask to take the next grade, or expect to receive it. A preoccupation with advancement is a manifestation of the self-important ego and that is something the practice of taekwondo attempts to suppress; for it is only when the ego is diminished that the practitioner can truly behave without self-interest.

There will be times when the student feels he cannot master a technique. This is inevitable, given the high demands made by taekwondo upon the abilities of every practitioner. The student who will eventually succeed to the highest levels of self-achievement is the one who is able to persevere; the student with motivation to push himself through all hardship and obstacles. The naturally competent student is at as much disadvantage spiritually as he is gifted physically. Being able to perform even difficult techniques without problem means that he does not develop the resilience that allows him to bounce back from the inevitable obstruction. Surprisingly, very few gifted students ever make it to black belt.

Courage is another essential ingredient for the taekwondo student. There are those who feel daunted by the prospect of sparring or destruction techniques. Apprehension is natural and tempers otherwise reckless aggression, but actual fear can inhibit performance. The student must try to conquer himself if he expects to succeed against others.

Mastering taekwondo

It is possible to become a master of technique and yet not master taekwondo. The novice learns the patterns, basic moves and combinations and, by the time he has reached black belt, he has achieved a high degree of competence in them. He can demonstrate any one technique with poise, balance and power. His techniques are strong enough to break boards and shatter bricks yet, at this stage, he has only completed his apprenticeship. To become a true master, he must now systematically 'forget' all he has learned. His mind must be freed from contemplation of technical things and left unclouded to react naturally.

During the learning process, the right and wrong ways to perform a technique are identified. The student concentrates on getting each move correct and, during the performance of a pattern, he will take pains to ensure the moves are performed with the correct fluidity, power and rhythm. After many years of such intense practice, the body learns what is required of it and begins to move as though of itself. The Master is freed of the preoccupation of choosing between the right and wrong – the right way comes instinctively.

The conscious mind becomes uninvolved with the mere mechanism of taekwondo and delegates that to the unconscious mind. The effect of this is to make responses immeasurably faster and more correctly.

When the hand is inadvertently placed on a hot surface, the fingers sense the heat and a nerve message flashes through the spinal cord in a reflex arc that jerks the hand away. There is no conscious deliberation of the sensation and the train of events needed to remove the hand from danger. In exactly the same way, the taekwondo Master does not consciously recognize and select an appropriate counter to an attack. He does so without thinking and very much faster than the expert in technique. Many advanced students and even black belts sometimes find themselves sparring with a Master who seems to anticipate and nullify their every move. Such a person has developed the empty mind needed to master taekwondo.

Training

The place for training in taekwondo is known as the *dojang*, or 'place of training in the way'. When entering it, the student and teacher will show their commitment to the objects of taekwondo by pausing at the door and performing a standing bow towards the teacher. If the teacher is not present, the bow will be made to the senior student or simply to the centre of the training hall. This bow should not be skimped – just as respect should never be. The pause is distinct and the body brought to a formal attention stance with the hands clasped into fists. The head and upper body is inclined forward, held for a second at its lowest position and then brought back upright again (**figure 1**). After that, the student may enter the dojang proper.

Figure 1 Standing bow

Once inside he must behave with decorum. He must not smoke, talk loudly or laugh. When sitting, he should rest his back against the wall and tuck his feet up so no one can trip over them. Under no circumstances should he lie or sprawl out across the floor. During training, there should be no chatter at all and the only sound heard is that of the teacher giving commands or making corrections. During pair-form sparring, it is permissible for the partners to converse in a low voice in order to agree coordination of moves but this should not rise above an unobtrusive level.

Students wishing to leave the class during training must first get the permission of the teacher. They may neither enter nor leave without his approval and, each time they go out or come in, they must pause and perform the standing bow. Those who come in late should exercise until warm, then bow to the teacher and remain standing until called to join the class.

At the beginning of training, the teacher will call the class to order. He will stand at the front and students will line up according to grade, with the seniors down one side and in parallel lines of descending competence. Once the lines are correctly dressed, the class comes to attention stance and bows in unison to the teacher.

The teacher then conducts a formal warm-up series of exercises. These gradually raise the condition of the body from normal to the level required to meet the demands of arduous training. There are two types of exercise, the first being those which exercise the muscles through running or jumping on the spot, press-ups, trunk curls etc., and the second being stretching exercises which take the warmed muscles through the limit of their extension.

Basic techniques

Basic techniques consist of single punches, kicks, strikes, or blocks performed to the instructor's count. Each time he shouts, one technique is performed. As it trains, the class will gradually advance along the wooden floor of the dojang until a natural limit is reached. At that time the teacher will call for a turn and the class performs it in unison. The basic techniques practised may vary from line to line. The senior students may well be given a more complicated technique while the novices concentrate on something less demanding. After the syllabus requirements have been covered, the class will move on to combination technique. This links several basic techniques together in a logical sequence and teaches continuity of movement.

Pair-form sparring

Pair-form sparring teaches the student the concept of distance and timing in a safe yet challenging way. At the outset, the class will perform multi-step sparring, with one line attacking by using three identical techniques. The defenders fall back from the attack and respond with three identical defences but, following the third, a counter-attack is employed. As standards improve and the partners learn to move together, emphasis shifts to single-step sparring, with a realistic attack being met by an immediate response. Although the attack is known beforehand, it can be delivered without warning and simulates controlled free sparring.

Pattern training uses whole chains of combinations to teach the student technique, speed and agility. Each pattern has a different emphasis or purpose and together they incorporate most of the techniques found in taekwondo. The first patterns are simple series of elementary techniques but later forms become steadily more complicated and involved.

Free sparring

Free sparring in the class consists of pairs of partners using unprogrammed techniques against each other. Despite the freedom of action inherent in this training, certain techniques and targets are prohibited in the interests of safety. Attacks to the eyes with open-hand techniques are not allowed. Also prohibited are punches to the face and attacks to the groin. The free sparring may use controlled contact or rely upon the use of body armour. Controlled contact means that techniques are pulled short of hard impact. This requires great power of concentration and one lapse can have painful results.

Body armour allows full power strikes to be made to the body but care must be exercised when sparring partners are of unequal weight. The heavier partner has a responsibility to ensure he doesn't hurt his lighter opponent. Similarly, higher grades must be careful not to injure the lower grade. The less-experienced athlete cannot be expected to behave rationally when free sparring and care must be taken to avoid unintentionally injuring him. Shin guards and forearm pads are useful for reducing bruising and gumshields are a wise precaution. To work effectively, these must be obtained from a dentist after an impression of the teeth and gums has been taken. Proprietary gumshields are often worse than useless. Boxes should also be worn by male competitors. These must be of the type worn by boxers rather than the simple plastic cup slipped inside the underpants or jockstrap. The cup can move about during kicks and trap parts of the genitals outside. A hard bang on the displaced cup can cause severe injuries.

Competition is a form of free sparring in which the techniques are assessed for their scoring value. Since there is no limit to the power which can be used against the body, weight categories are employed and body armour is mandatory. Scores are recorded by a panel of four corner judges and fighting is under the direction of a central referee. A jury oversees the operation of the match and ensures that the rules are properly observed.

Destruction techniques are practised under close supervision and are in any case denied to children. The taekwondo athlete must be able to demonstrate power and the breaking of a specified thickness of boards is one way of assessing that power. It is a fact that destruction practice does point up weaknesses in technique that cannot otherwise be revealed. Before allowing the student to begin training in destruction technique, the teacher will ensure that the body weapons to be used are adequately conditioned and, further, that the thickness of board selected does not exceed the student's abilities. To practise for impact techniques, the student uses an impact pad held by another student, or a punching post. Practice with either of these will indicate any shortcoming.

Grading

The student's competence in these various elements of taekwondo training is assessed at periodic intervals by means of the grading examination. The student must complete the assigned syllabus for his grade under the watchful eye of a grading examiner and, if he is successful, his personal training record is endorsed at the new grade reached and a different coloured belt may be worn. The colour of the belt identifies the level of competence reached, or kup grade, and the following is a typical coloured-belt sequence:

10th Kup	White belt	9th Kup	White with yellow tab
8th Kup	Yellow belt	7th Kup	Yellow with green tab
6th Kup	Green belt	5th Kup	Green with blue tab
4th Kup	Blue belt	3rd Kup	Blue with red tab
2nd Kup	Red belt	1st Kup	Red with black tab
	1st Dan	Black belt	

The average interval between the kup grades is three to four months calculated on the basis of two training sessions per week. Once black belt has been reached, the progression continues but with longer intervals between successive dan grades. There is a minimum period of eighteen months between first and second dan, two years between second and third dan and a minimum of two to three years between third and fourth dan. The grading examiner for the kup grades must be at least fifth dan. He is entitled to grade up to and including third dan. Above this, a panel of seventh dans is required. The theoretical highest dan grade which can be achieved is ninth dan.

CHAPTER 3: DEVELOPING FORCE IN TAEKWONDO TECHNIQUES

All martial arts require a measure of physical effort to execute their techniques. Those which depend upon throwing, holding and locking use the principle of force applied to vulnerable areas of the opponent by means of leverages. Impact-based martial arts such as taekwondo rely upon powerful punches, kicks and strikes to incapacitate. The impact force is generated by a fast-moving weapon colliding with a vulnerable target.

Taekwondo is justly famous for the amazing feats of breaking demonstrated by high grades. The edge of the hand is sufficient to break clean through a brick. A straight punch smashes through four inches of hardened wood. These achievements eloquently illustrate the successful application of impact theory within taekwondo. Its techniques focus maximum energy through concentration of attention and energy, coordination of musculature, correct stance and body movement. There are, however, serious drawbacks to giving a total physical commitment to one blow. If the blow should miss, there is a finite time while it is recovered and, during this, no other full-power blow can be launched. With the opponent refusing to stand still and be hit, the possibility of misses is quite high, so taekwondo technique must be a compromise between full commitment and speedy follow-up. Expressed simply, the taekwondo athlete must be able to hit hard and frequently, where the need arises.

Body Weapons

The body weapon used in taekwondo must be able to withstand injury, while inflicting it on the victim. It is pointless having a high-energy body weapon which fractures or sprains on impact. The conditioned weapon withstands greater impacts so it can be used on a wide variety of targets. Certain parts of the body are less sensitive to pain so, for maximum effect, the impact technique should be applied to a vulnerable area.

The weapon must be capable of acceleration if it is to develop impact. Acceleration is the rate of change of velocity from instant to instant. The weapon is initially at rest and has no energy value. The action of muscles acting through levers moves the weapon at a gradually increasing speed until maximum speed is reached. The higher this maximum speed, the greater energy potential the weapon has. A cricket ball resting on a pane of glass has little energy but, if it is dropped from a couple of metres, it accelerates under the force of gravity and acquires energy so that, when it encounters the pane, the latter breaks. It is as though the moving cricket ball has gained in weight.

The weapon must also have a reasonable mass if it is to be effective. The dried pea dropped upon a pane will not break it because, although the pea is accelerating at the same rate as the ball, it possesses insufficient mass. It is certainly possible to accelerate the pea to a high enough speed to break the glass but such acceleration exceeds the limits of the human body and so we are constrained to use larger weapons.

The body should always move behind any punch or kick. The punch which uses only the mass and muscles of the arm is less powerful than one with body weight behind it. For this reason, taekwondo techniques always involve a body movement. During a front kick, for example, the hips are suddenly thrust forward and the kick may be preceded by a short hop forwards. A punch is always accompanied by a step forwards or a transfer of body weight behind the blow.

When the falling object encounters the flat surface, it gives up its energy of movement (kinetic energy) in a fraction of a second. Some of the energy will be absorbed by the surface – which may then deform or shatter – and the remainder will be passed back into the object as recoil. The dried pea strikes the pane of glass and rebounds from it, simply because the energy it possesses is low. The cricket ball shatters the glass and does not rebound because its energy is sufficient to take the glass past its elastic limit. The weapon must develop sufficient energy to transmit force into the target, losing as little as possible through recoil. It achieves this either by travelling very fast or by having a substantial mass.

Recoil

The light person can literally bounce off his opponent unless he is able to absorb recoil. This can be done in two ways, the first using a static absorbtion method. Static absorbtion of recoil depends upon a rigid stance. During the lunge punch, the back leg locks straight at the same time as the punching elbow. If weight is concentrated over the front leg, the impact energy will not find an easy escape back through the attacker. To test your ability to absorb recoil, stand in lunge punch stance and lock your arm and back leg. Then have a partner move forward until your fist is pressing against his chest. Then have him continue pushing forwards while you resist. You will find that, if there is insufficient weight on your front leg, it will rise. If your front arm is not locked straight, the elbow will gradually bend. Similarly, if you have raised the heel of your back foot or bent the propping knee, you will be driven back onto it.

When using a system of static absorbtion, it is therefore very necessary to become perfectly rigid at the moment of impact, concentrating all your force on one point and tightening up the whole body. The punching arm has to become a straight rod with the bones of the upper arm in alignment with those of the lower, right through the chain of carpals, metacarpals and knuckles. Any kink in this straight line will cause loss of impact through flexing. Such a system is ideal for smashing through blocks of wood held immovable, but it is too rigid for sparring.

Kinetic absorbtion of recoil uses the energy of the moving body to resist wasteful losses on impact. If the body is moving quickly behind a blow, the stance is of little importance. The sheer momentum of the strike absorbs recoil and it makes no difference even if the attacker is standing on one leg.

The characteristics of the target also determine the effect of an impact. If the target is rigid, the energy of impact is given up in an instant and a shockwave capable of breaking wood, tiles and bones results. If the target is absorbent, impact energy is shed less violently though injuries to soft tissues can still result from a powerful blow. It is therefore important not to aim all the energy of a blow at one level. Such a blow retains its maximum effect only so long as the target doesn't move.

Impact

Any attempt to bring a technique to a premature end before it has developed its full potential will adversely affect its power. In a jab, for example, care must be taken to allow full impact before the fist is withdrawn. If the punch makes contact just as it is being braked prior to retrieval, it will have spent most of its energy.

The technique must be accelerating at the moment of impact. Once the arm or leg has straightened fully, the limit of range is reached and the blow sheds energy. Range is therefore a vital consideration when developing maximum force. If the target is too close, the weapon may not have the necessary distance over which to accelerate to its maximum potential. In this case, the punch can be exchanged for an elbow strike, the latter needing less distance in which to build up energy. Kicks are generally better over longer ranges whereas punches operate best at a medium distance.

The limbs are the weapons of the body. The head is not used because of the risk of injury to the face and because frequent heavy impacts on the head lead to cumulative brain damage. The arms and legs can be accelerated sharply and are massive enough to develop adequate kinetic energy. The arms are light in relation to their musculature and so can be accelerated more quickly. Although the legs normally cannot move at the same speed, they generate more impact energy because they have a greater mass and, within the limits of the human body, mass is more important than acceleration. To be sure, a lighter person striking quickly can develop a great deal of energy but not nearly so much as a really large person punching at the same speed.

Whether a kick or a punch is used, the object will be to deliver the maximum of force into a small area. Large weapons – such as the sole of the foot or the entire fist – are wasteful because they have a large area of contact and impact energy is spread thinly over the whole surface. The same energy channelled through just two knuckles or the ball of the foot will have a greater effect because it is concentrated into a small area. Therefore, all the weapons of taekwondo present a small-contact area allied with the ability to withstand high impacts.

The high-powered punch

The weapon itself may be enhanced by some simple actions. The punch, for example, is rotated on impact with the target. This rotation is made by the muscles of the lower arm and, if the alignment of bones is correct, the two large knuckles rotate without describing an arc. This rotation adds energy to the punch and can also tear the opponent's skin. The fully formed fist takes a great deal of muscular energy to maintain and this causes the lower arm to become rigid. This inhibits the speed to which the arm can be accelerated and so it is a good idea to leave the fist only loosely clenched until it is about to land. At that moment, it is suddenly tightened. This has the effect of making the arm more rigid and the punch more effective.

The mechanism of the high-energy punch requires that the uninvolved muscles be as relaxed as possible so as not to inhibit the natural movement of the body. At the moment of impact, breath is expelled violently and all the muscles of the body are locked up tight. This all-over muscle spasm makes the body more rigid and increases its potential for absorbing recoil. The sharp exhalation of breath tenses the abdominal muscles and makes them more resistant to impact. With a little practice, the stomach can be tensed to the point where it can accept very hard punches and kicks without injury. The exhalation must originate from contraction of the diaphragm, otherwise it is ineffective.

To augment the power of a punch, as many complementary muscles as can be used are harnessed. Thus the reverse punch will begin with a hip-twist that takes the punching hip forwards while leaving the punch cocked and waiting (figures 2, 3). Hip-rotation causes a twisting of the spine and, when this reaches a peak, the punching shoulder and arm are driven forward and the elbow begins to straighten (figure 4). The muscles used in the punch are those of the arm and upper chest, yet, by staging the lead-in to the punch, the more powerful muscles of the hips and abdomen can be brought into play.

The coordinated movement is very complex. The hip does not rotate fully before the shoulder is released, otherwise the punch would proceed in a series of jerks. The take-over from the hips is smooth and accomplished while the hip is still accelerating. The action of the shoulder is enhanced by allowing it to move forwards from the rest position, behind the advancing arm. The shoulders work in unison so it follows that, while one side is advancing, the other is being pulled back. For this reason, the high-energy punch incorporates a fast pull-back of the non-punching arm. The speed of withdrawal must precisely match that of the punching arm if the shoulders are to swing freely. Novices should be encouraged to concentrate on withdrawing the non-punching arm rather than on making the punch itself.

Figure 2 A powerful reverse punch begins with a hip-twist

At the start of reverse punch, the stance can have any weight distribution. On delivery, however, it must be concentrated over the front leg and moving forward as the punch connects; otherwise the stance itself is not too important (figure 4). If there is no opportunity to move forward, then the stance assumes a very real importance and must have great longitudinal stability.

The punching arm must be straightening as it makes contact. Body movement alone carries the punch deep into its target. If the elbow is bent during impact, it will waste energy through recoil. Furthermore, its effective mass will be seriously reduced since there will not be the full weight of the arm and body behind it.

The snap punch off the front fist is a shorter movement but still amounts to more than just using the muscles of the arm and shoulder. The action begins in the hips, with body weight moving forward over the front foot while the hip on the punching side twists forwards. The fist is held loose and, just before the punch is to be launched, the other fist moves forward slightly and then pulls back abruptly. This small movement allows the punching shoulder to swing freely

Figure 3 . . . causing the rear heel to lift off and taking weight forwards

Figure 4 The punching shoulder and arm follow the hip forward

behind the punch. Synchronization of the punch is important, with the arm well extended by the time the hip has twisted fully forward.

The Powerful Kick

The kick accelerates over a greater distance and produces much more energy than the punch. The muscles of the leg are more powerful but are slower acting. The orthodox front snap kick, for example, consists of two phases. The first is an active accelerating phase and the second is a passive flicking out of the accelerated lower limb. The main development of force in the kick is therefore restricted to the first phase, when the muscles of the upper leg are drawing the rear leg forwards and up. As the knee approaches the correct height, its movement is braked and the lower leg flies out under the influence of momentum into the target. If the knee is allowed to reach the correct height before the lower leg begins to extend, then the energy built up will be shed and the lower leg will have to be driven into the target by muscular effort alone.

The side thrust kick (**figure 5**) uses a different approach with no passive flicking of the foot. As the kicking knee is rising to the correct height, the lower leg is driven into the target like a piston. The kick is

Figure 5 The side thrust kick, strengthened by hip twist and body lean for balance

strengthened by the hips twisting and the supporting leg pivotting, so body weight is added to the thrust. All too easily the kick can degenerate into a powerful shove, so leave the kicking leg relaxed until it is just about to land and is approaching maximum speed, then tighten up all your muscles and breathe out in a sharp gasp.

The turning kick is a coordinated series of movements beginning with the upper body twisting in the direction of the kick. This is the reverse of a punch initiation where the hips lead the shoulders. The torsion in the spine tends to pull the kicking hip forwards and weight lifts off the rear foot, allowing it to rise. The supporting leg swivels and the kicking knee comes up and around, describing a rising circular path that ends with the knee pointing directly at the target. As the knee is reaching the correct height, the kicking hip rises up and over the hip of the supporting leg and the lower leg is driven out. The back is arched and, at the moment of impact, the body is 'Y' shaped, with the supporting leg holding up the trunk which is leaning one way and the kicking leg the other. For maximum power, the turning kick harnesses the force of gravity. The kicking knee is allowed to rise above the height of the target so the kick descends in a shallow arc to the target.

CHAPTER 4:
THE STANCES OF
TAEKWONDO

To deliver an effective strike or block, it is necessary to be at the right distance from the opponent and able to use the counter-attacks of choice without delay. This requires a mastery of stance. Though a stance may be held for only a fraction of a second, it provides the correct arrangement of balance, position and technique availability. If the stance is poor, then all that stems from it will be flawed. The punch will lose its energy and possibly miss altogether; the kick will be off balance and vulnerable and the block will prove less effective. More importantly, the athlete will be caught off guard more frequently.

The Kinds of Stance
The stance may be general or highly specialized. Generalized stances have an even weight distribution and offer the maximum alternatives in direction of movement and deployment of techniques. Specialized stances favour certain techniques and are normally held for only a short time while that technique is in use. They are unwieldly and do not lend themselves to alternative use. Stance heights vary. Some are upright with nearly straight knees and others are low and long. The higher stances are more mobile and lead to faster movements but the user can be driven out of the competition area under a fierce attack. Lower stances are naturally resistant to sudden attacks and allow the user to dig in under pressure. What they lose in speed and mobility, they gain in power.

The overall stability of a stance depends upon its weight distribution, height, length and width. Lower stances are more stable than taller ones. An even weight distribution gives a less polarized centre of gravity and a long stance makes for stability in the direction of its length though rapid movement may be slowed. A wide stance, too, gives stability but can expose the groin to attack. Thus a general-purpose stance will be of medium height and even weight distribution. It will be long enough to provide stability and wide enough to provide balance but without opening the groin to attack. If the front foot is turned in slightly and the body set at a slight angle, the groin is covered against direct attack.

In some stances the feet are flat on the floor, in others one or both feet may be raised at the heel. In higher

24

and faster stances, the main weight rests on the balls of the feet, allowing rapid movement without dragging. The attitude of the body is also affected by stance. In forward stance it is turned square on, and in straddle stance fully sideways on. The first provides the opponent with a large area for attack, and the other with the smallest area. Nevertheless the straddle stance is specialized and allows only a small repertoire of techniques to be used from it without modification. In fighting stance, the body is turned three-quarters on to the opponent so the opportunity for counter-attack is reduced without limiting the body weapons which can be used.

Movement between stances must be fluid and quick. If the opponent is moving back quickly, it is necessary to maintain pressure of attack by advancing. If the opponent opens the attack, the defender must be able to retreat with a valid defence. During any taekwondo match there are innumerable shifts in stance and distance. The latter must be constantly maintained so it is optimal for the techniques being employed. Knowledge of stance will allow adjustments to be made without exposing weaknesses or hesitations upon which the opponent can capitalize.

Figure 6 Attention stance

Attention stance

Attention stance is a formal stance used at the beginning and end of training exercises (figure 6). It is not used to deliver techniques but is a relaxed and prepared stance assumed when the opponent is well outside of attacking distance. The body is upright and the head held high. The back is straight and the arms hang naturally, close to the sides of the body. The hands are closed into fists. The muscles of the stomach are relaxed and the weight allowed to sink down. The legs are straight and the heels touch with feet directed outwards at a 45 degree angle.

The feet can be brought together for a variety of attention stance known as closed stance. This often follows formal attention stance and marks the beginning of a training programme such as a pattern. As before, the arms hang to the sides and end in closed fists, but in some schools the arms are held slightly away from the body and bend slightly at the elbows, to give a bowed appearance.

Ready stance

There are various forms of ready stance but the most common has the feet a shoulder-width apart (measured between their outer edges) and parallel. The stance is fairly stable in a side-to-side direction because the body weight is resting on a wide base (figure 7). It is not,

Figure 7 The most common form of ready stance, with feet a shoulder-width apart and parallel

Figure 8 Walking stance.

Figure 9 Fighting stance. The knees are slightly bent and the weight distributed evenly on the balls of both feet

however, resistant to shoves from the front and back. In some styles the feet are turned out slightly, and in others they are turned in. From ready stance, first the left leg moves to the side, then the right. When returning from ready stance to attention stance, this sequence is reversed. The fists are brought across the front of the body and there is a general tightening up in readiness for impending action. This stance is used immediately prior to an attacking or defending move and is taken up when the opponent has moved a little closer but is still outside effective range.

Natural stance

Natural stance is a development of ready stance to be adopted in anticipation of an attack. The back remains straight with the head held high and the fists carried at the front of the body in front of the thighs. Either one of the feet slides forward a full step and finishes with the heel of the advanced foot in line with the toes of the other. When the foot is moved forwards, it is not lifted from the floor. The stance retains its natural width and fore-and-aft stability is improved because of the lengthened footbase (distance between the heels).

If the leading foot is taken forwards so that the heel is now a full step ahead of the toes of the rear foot, walking stance is formed (**figure 8**). There is more bodyweight on the front foot than on the back and the heels are in line. The front foot faces forwards and the rear foot is turned slightly outwards. The knees are bent a little and a defensive guard is carried. If the left leg is advanced, the left arm is raised to shoulder height and the fist closed. There is a 90 degree bend in the elbow of the leading arm and the forearm comes to lie well out and slightly across the front of the body. The other fist is raised to just below the chin with the elbow kept close to the body. In this position, the arms can be used effectively for both attack and defence.

Walking stance

Walking stance is quite a useful general purpose stance well suited to conditions requiring rapid movement in all directions. The body is slightly turned away from the attacker, thus reducing the targets vulnerable to attack. Fighting stance is a further development of walking stance, being a well-guarded high and unspecialized stance. The knees are slightly bent and weight is distributed evenly on the balls of the feet. This stance is most commonly used during sparring practice (**figure 9**).

Semi-forward stance

Semi-forward stance is intermediate between walking

stance and forward stance. The footbase is slightly greater than one step and the heels are in line. Both feet are flat on the floor with a weight bias over the front leg. The knees are well bent so the centre of gravity is lowered. The back is straight and the head is held high. In this stance, the athlete can attack square on with either a punch or a block.

Forward stance

Forward stance (**figure 10**) is a logical progression from semi-forward stance and is achieved by extending the leading foot so the footbase has a length of one and a half steps. The feet maintain a width equivalent to that of the shoulders so there is also a lateral stability. The front foot is forward facing and the rear foot is rotated outwards. The outward rotation of the rear foot is minimal. If it is too much, the hips are not able to face fully forwards. The front knee bears down directly over the instep of the leading foot and the leg should neither be bowed out or in. The rear knee is locked straight and both feet are flat on the ground.

The beginner finds it difficult to achieve the correct degree of side step, especially after stepping from stance to stance. The advancing foot tends to sweep inwards and side step is lost. This robs the stance of its lateral stability and leads to unsteadiness. The beginner also finds it a problem to keep the back leg locked straight and, the more the rear leg is turned forwards, the more difficult that task becomes. The novice must ·always ensure that his feet are not at right angles to each other.

The shoulders must not be hunched and the body should not lean in any particular direction. The stance can be tested by trying to push the holder off balance by pressing against his chest, or by drawing forward one of his arms. Although lateral stability is not especially high, it should be possible to absorb some minor shoves or pulls. Forward stance is specialized for powerful forwards and backwards movements.

Figure 10 Forward stance, achieved by extending the leading foot so the footbase has a length of one and a half steps

Back stance

Back stance (**figure 11**) can be formed from forward stance by drawing back the front foot until there is a distance of one good step between the toes of the rear foot and the heel of the front foot. Weight is transferred back over the rear foot so the hip comes to lie above the bent supporting knee. The knee in turn is directly above the toes of the rear foot. The front leg bends naturally according to the length of the stance and the leading foot faces forwards and lies flat on the floor. The rear foot is turned outwards at right angles and most of the body weight descends on it. The hips are turned 45 degrees away from the front.

Figure 11 Back stance involves a shift of body weight towards the rear

The novice may experience difficulty in getting the centre of gravity over his rear leg and push his backside out. This is incorrect – the body must be perfectly upright if it is to allow techniques to develop their maximum potential. Sometimes, too, the front leg straightens and this reduces the speed at which front leg kicks can be used.

Advancing stance

Advancing stance is a curious reversal of back stance in which most weight is placed on the front leg and the rear heel is lifted, leaving only the ball of the foot in contact. This stance has the same footbase as back stance but is polarized for a sudden fast advance instead of the tactical retreat often associated with back stance. Advancing stance uses the back leg to force the body forwards and the weight on the front foot acts as a brake preventing this movement.

Tiger stance

Tiger stance (**figure 12**) is developed from back stance by withdrawing the leading foot until it is slightly less than one step in front. Weight is transferred entirely over the rear foot and the supporting knee bent. The front knee is also bent and the heel of the leading foot lifted clear of the floor. The feet are slightly less than 90 degrees to each other with the front foot turned in very slightly and the thighs brought together to close the groin against attack. Since so little weight rests on the front foot, it can be quickly deployed as a kick or fend-off.

Figure 12 A further shift of body weight and drawing back the front foot leads to tiger stance

Crane stance

Lifting the front foot completely clear of the floor leads to crane stance. This is a transient stance, held for a fraction of a second and used to avoid a sweep to the front foot or to deliver a kick. The supporting leg remains bent and is slightly turned outwards. The supported leg is also bent and the foot is pressed to the side of the supporting knee or hooked behind the knee joint.

X-stance

X-stance is another transient stance, and is used during an advance from one straddle stance to another. Start in left straddle stance and bring your right foot across and over the instep of the left as you step through. By keeping the feet close together, the calf of the right leg jams against the front of the left shin. This configuration is useful for following up with a side kick. Alternatively, the right foot can pass behind the left, causing a stronger hip-turn that can be utilized by a follow-up back kick. The step must be made on the ball of the foot.

During the step through x-stance, the body must be kept upright and the hips pressed forwards. The knees remain flexed so the body does not bob up and down. The x-stance is also used during a strong advance when weight is thrown forward from an advancing, walking, or forward stance. The rear leg is quickly drawn up behind and the shin jams against the back of the calf of the leading leg. The heel of the rear foot lifts clear of the floor. From this position it is possible to deliver a strong lower x-block or vertical back fist to the face.

Straddle stance

Straddle stances (**figure 13**) are suitable for lateral movements. They have little stability in a forwards or back situation but are ideal for launching side kicks. The width of stance can vary but it is generally one and a half shoulder widths. The feet slightly diverge, the knees bend and are forced outwards so that each comes to lie directly above the middle of the instep. The heels of both feet lie on one straight line. The back is kept straight and the bottom pulled in. The hips are projected forwards and lifted.

Figure 13 Straddle stance has great sideways stability; the weight is evenly distributed

Getting Stances Right

The beginner may find difficulty in getting the weight directly above the feet and often novices adopt a stance where the knees have collapsed inwards. This can be remedied by reducing the width of the stance.

If one foot is advanced forwards, so that the heel of the leading foot is in line with the toes of the other, a curious tension stance called hourglass stance results. Many Europeans use the shoulders and chest too much in the generation of power and that which comes from the stomach is more suitable for taekwondo purposes. The hourglass stance was originally developed to realize this power and the athlete trained to withstand unsettling shoves, pushes and heavy blows from the opponent. This stance is hardly ever seen in modern taekwondo because emphasis is placed on fast movements and evasion.

In stances where there is an equal weight distribution, one stance can translate into another with a simple step. Where there is an unequal distribution, the centre of gravity must be moved before a step can take place. Thus, in tiger stance or back stance, weight must be transferred onto the forward foot before the step can take place. The lifted front foot of tiger stance is pressed to the floor and weight brought over it while keeping the body upright and the face back from trouble. The back leg then advances past and stops when it reaches

Figure 14 Begin a turn from forward stance

its final position. Weight is retained over the new rear leg so the character of the stance is preserved. It is important to keep the correct width as well as length of stance.

Forward stance requires a little practice to avoid bobbing up and down and narrowing width during the step. The rear foot is advanced past the front and slides over the floor in a straight line which maintains the correct side step for the stance. When it has travelled the correct distance, it stops and weight is settled through the ball of the foot. Fighting, semi-forward and walking stance are advanced in the same way.

Straddle stance uses x-stance to advance or retreat. The advancing leg passes either in front of or behind the forward foot. The back must be kept straight, the bottom tucked in and there should be no tendency to lean the body during the step.

Turns

Turns are ways of quickly facing threats from new directions. In an unspecialized stance with an even weight distribution, a turn can be accomplished by stepping across with the back leg and swivelling the hips (**figures 14, 15, 16**). The back leg moves across because the lateral component of the stance must be maintained. If the back foot is slid too far across, the new stance will be very wide and open to immediate counter-attack. Only regular practice will show the correct degree of side step to be taken.

When stepping to the side, the leg is bent and the heel raised. This lessens the effect of dragging and allows a faster turn. The body remains forward facing for as long as possible since the energy for the turn is generated in the hips and not the shoulders. As the hips continue to rotate, a tension is built up in the spine. This is released when the upper body begins to swing around behind. As the hips turn fully on, weight settles on both feet and the back leg straightens. Remember always to look behind before turning and you will not be caught unprepared.

If the turn is a right angle instead of a complete rotation, the front foot moves to the side. It is kept bent and weight taken on the ball of the foot. As soon as it reaches the final position, the hips rotate and the body turns to face the new direction. The angle the body turns to is determined by the position of the front foot.

A turn from straddle stance is easily achieved by simply twisting the upper torso to face in the new direction. Back stance and tiger stance turns are made by sliding the front foot across and then smoothly transferring weight over it as the body swivels to the new direction.

Figure 15 Step across with the rear foot and make the blocking arm ready

Figure 16 Swivel the hips to face the new direction and reform forward stance

CHAPTER 5: THE WEAPONS OF TAEKWONDO

Taekwondo is a martial art which depends upon impact. Therefore its weapons must possess sufficient mass and energy to cause damage to the opponent. More than this, they must be able to do so without themselves being injured. In order to develop energy, they must be capable of acceleration and have sufficient distance over which to travel. They are most effective when as much as possible of the impact energy is transferred into the target without undue loss. Significantly better effects will accrue if this energy is transmitted through a small area of contact – this leads to a more penetrating blow.

In practice, the major weapons are those of the hands and feet. To use the body's weapons to their full potential, they must be properly conditioned. The unconditioned fist, for example, may not be able to close fully so the middle joints of the fingers rap painfully against hard targets. The knuckles themselves are shielded by a thin layer of skin. A hard impact can rip the skin and bruise the bone. The wrist can flex violently on impact and sprain or fracture.

Weapons of the Hand
Despite these disadvantages, the fist remains the most often-used hand weapon. It can be used in a number of ways but the most usual is a swing or straight punch with the front of the knuckles acting as impact surfaces (**figure 17**). To concentrate the power of the punch in a small area, the impact is made through the knuckles of the index and middle finger only. To form the fist, extend your fingers and open the thumb out from the palm. Then bend the fingers forwards until their tips come to rest on the pad of flesh that runs along the top of the palm. Close the fist fully and fold the thumb across the middle of the two closest fingers.

Make sure the thumb does not protrude because it can easily get caught in loose clothing. Do not wrap the thumb up inside the fingers because a hard impact may dislocate it. If the two major knuckles are to be the first to contact the target, it is necessary to make sure the lower joints of the fingers do not project forwards. The objective is to make a right-angle bend which pulls the fingers out of the way. The way to achieve this is to do press-ups on the fists and to practise with a punching pad. The latter is very useful because it confirms

Figure 17 A straight punch uses the front of the knuckles as impact surfaces

whether there is a straight line from the bones of the lower arm, through the wrist bones, to the knuckles themselves. If there is such a line, the fist will not flex on impact.

When using the fist in the manner of an orthodox punch, it is customary to rotate the forearm just before impact. Start with the palm of your fist pointing upwards and, as it is about to land, turn it palm down. This action makes the punch more effective and can cause laceration of the opponent's skin. The rotation is made around the knuckles and they themselves do not move in an arc.

The back of the fist can also be used as a weapon. The impact area is still the two large knuckles, but their upper surface, rather than the front. Back fist is a very fast and long-range hand technique which works well against the side of the face or the nose.

Upright back fist

An upright back fist is best delivered stepping forward into an x-stance, where the shin of the rear leg presses against the calf of the other. The striking forearm is held vertically and the other in a closed fist guard, near the elbow. As the forward movement of the body comes to a stop, the striking forearm is driven out towards the opponent's face and drawn back just as quickly. This sudden reversal of motion causes the back fist to tip forward on the loose wrist and strike the opponent on the bridge of the nose.

Horizontal back fist

There are two ways of delivering a horizontal back fist. The first is best delivered from a fighting stance. Weight is transferred to the front leg and the striking arm rises until the elbow is pointing directly at the target. The hips then turn away from the direction of the strike, which is lashed out horizontally into the side of the face. As the elbow straightens, it is just as quickly withdrawn, and this whip-lash action causes the fist to snap out and back.

The second uses the pull-back of the non-striking arm to power the technique. To practise, stand in a back stance and withdraw the striking fist so it overlies the opposite shoulder (**figure 18**). Extend the non-striking arm forwards and pull it back strongly. As you do, unroll the striking arm and let it lash out into the target (**figure 19**). The back fist makes contact as the withdrawing arm comes to a stop on the hip.

Back fist

Back fist is difficult to practise because the fist must be tightly closed on impact and this tends to tense the

Figure 18 Horizontal back fist, using the pull-back of the non-striking arm to power the technique

Figure 19 The impact area of back fist is the upper surface of the knuckles

wrist so a full whip-lash is not possible.

Hammer fist uses the orthodox fist configuration but strikes in such a way as to impact on the pad of flesh that runs between the base of the little finger and the wrist. The fist must be closed tightly on impact, otherwise the fingers jar painfully together. It is also important to strike directly on the pad of flesh and not on either the little finger joint or the wrist.

Hammer fist

Hammer fist can be used as a strike or as a block. As a strike it is directed downwards like a club, or sideways into the target. To strike downwards, the fist is raised high above the head and swung downwards. Its action is strengthened by pulling back the other arm which is normally kept open until the hammer fist is about to impact. At this instant, both fists tighten up spasmodically. Use is also made of the body weight and, just before the blow lands, the knees are suddenly bent.

Horizontal strike

A horizontal strike is best performed from straddle stance. The striking arm begins from a palm-up position on the opposite side of the chest. The striking arm swings around and the elbow begins to straighten. As it does, the palm of the striking hand rotates palm downwards and clenches tightly. The other arm closely follows the movement of the striking fist and thereby strengthens it.

Other techniques

Blocking techniques using hammer fist normally start with the little finger side of the fist touching the opposite side of the chest. The other arm extends well forward and is strongly drawn back to give the blocking movement more power. The blocking arm swings down and across the body and, just as it is about to make contact, rotates little finger outwards (**figure 20**). Hammer fist can also be used to strike down onto an attacking technique and, used in this way, is particularly effective against the opponent's elbow joint.

If the index finger is protruded from the fist, a one-knuckle punch is formed. The protruding knuckle is locked out by the thumb pressing directly on or behind .it. Another version protrudes the middle finger knuckle and jams it out by forcing together the lower joints of the flanking fingers. Although one-knuckle punch is not used a great deal, it is a very effective technique and concentrates force very efficiently. As a rule it is used against softer targets, though, if properly conditioned, it can prove a powerful weapon effective on any target.

If the fist is partially unrolled, impact can be made

Figure 20 Hammer fist used as a block

Figure 21 Palm heel is safe to use against bony targets

with the middle joints of the fingers against softer targets. Half-open fist is very rarely seen. If in this position the wrist is bent back, impact can be made with the heel of the palm. Palm heel is a very effective weapon against any target (**figure 21**). The troublesome problem of wrist flexion encountered with the orthodox front punch is ruled out and the padding over the palm heel makes bruising less of a problem. The thumb must be kept tightly tucked in since it can so easily be dislocated by catching it in jacket sleeves, etc.

Knife hand

If the hand is fully opened, further weapons become available. The most obvious perhaps is the knife hand. This technique delivers its impact through the narrow strip of muscle running along the edge of the palm between the base of the little finger and the wrist. The fingers must be rigidly extended on impact or they will be painfully jarred. The thumb folds and overlays the other edge of the palm.

Orthodox knife hand travels horizontally and the fingers cup slightly on impact. To practise it, stand in left fighting stance and pull the left hand back with the elbow bent, almost as though you were saluting. Extend the non-striking arm around the front of your chest with the elbow pointing towards the opponent (**figure 22**). Keep your upper body square on but rotate your hips clockwise so a torsion is set up in the spine. Instants later release your shoulders and strongly withdraw the right arm, pulling it to the hip. Use this motion to pull the knife hand around palm forward until it is about to connect, then suddenly scoop little finger upwards with it (**figure 23**, overleaf).

Figure 22 To practise knife hand, stand in left fighting stance and pull the left hand back with the elbow bent

Figure 23 Twist hips and strike to neck

Figure 24 From straddle stance, lean . . .

Knife hand can also be practised in a different way from right straddle stance. Lean the body away and take the striking hand over the opposite shoulder. Extend the other hand across the chest (**figure 24**). Transfer body weight back to the mid-line and withdraw the non-striking arm strongly. Use this to strengthen the knife strike as it moves into the target. As it is about to land, the wrist is rotated so the hand turns palm down (**figure 25**).

Reverse knife hand

The other side of the open hand is reverse knife hand. This uses the base of the index finger joint in a swinging motion that carries the weapon around and into the target. The thumb must be pressed well into the palm. Lean back from a right fighting stance and swing both arms out and behind – the left palm up, the right palm down (**figure 26**). The hips are twisted into the target but the shoulders lag just long enough to build up spinal torsion. When they are released, the upper body swings around and the right arm is pulled strongly back to the right hip. The left hand sweeps around and, just on impact, twists palm down (**figure 27**). Reverse knife hand is particularly effective against the neck and the jaw.

The fingers

The extended fingers are used to attack vulnerable targets such as the groin, neck and face (**figure 28**). The middle finger can be bent, so its tip comes into line with

Figure 25 . . . then twist the hips, pull back the non-striking arm and strike knife hand

Figure 26 Use both arms for reverse knife hand

Figure 27 Pull back the non-striking arm on impact

the index and fourth fingers of the extended hand. In this way the impact area is strengthened and less likely to flex painfully on impact. If the fingers are properly conditioned, some quite amazing feats of wood-breaking can be demonstrated. The extended fingers are driven into the target in a straight line. The strike begins palm-up and rotates palm down on impact.

Sometimes all but two fingers are closed into the palm. The two remaining fingers – usually the middle and index – are then used to attack the eyes. Occasionally the extended index finger alone is used as a low-energy strike to vulnerable areas. If the thumb and tips of fingers are brought together, a curious weapon like a chicken's beak is formed. The back of the open hand may also serve as a weapon when swung sideways into the opponent's face as a form of back-handed slap. The back of the flexed wrist can be used in the same way.

The Elbow

The elbow is an excellent short-range weapon which can be used in a variety of ways. Stand in left forward stance and carry your guard in a relaxed fighting posture (**figure 29**, overleaf). Keep your overall height constant and glide quickly forward into right forward stance. As you are stepping, bring the right elbow up and around the front of the body while pushing the fist into the palm of your other hand (**figure 30**, overleaf). Time the movement so the point of your elbow reaches the opponent's face just as you come to a stop (**figure 31**, overleaf). Remember to hit the opponent with the

Figure 28 Extended fingers can be used to attack vulnerable targets.such as the neck

Figure 29 Front elbow from forward stance

Figure 30 Bring elbow up and around front

Figure 31 Time impact so the point of your elbow reaches its target just as you come to a stop

Figure 32 Lean back for a side elbow strike

Figure 33 Transfer weight behind the striking elbow to give it more power

tip of the elbow, since this will concentrate power over a small area. A forearm smash is not nearly so effective.

The elbow can also be used as a sideways strike. Start in a high straddle stance and take both arms away from the direction of impending movement (**figure 32**, overleaf). Transfer weight towards the target and slide out into a lower straddle stance. As you come to a stop, drive your elbow into the target (**figure 33**). As in the first example, the timing of the move is essential for full power development. If the elbow strike lands after the stance has changed, much momentum energy will be lost.

A descending elbow strike is useful at close distance against the doubled-up opponent. The striking arm is shot up vertically in the air with fingers extended. It is then brought violently down, elbow first, to the back of the opponent's neck or spine. To add power to the strike, the open hand is closed suddenly upon impact and the knees are bent, lending body weight to the blow.

An upwards-travelling elbow strike is effective against the opponent's jaw. Begin from left fighting stance and swivel your hips anti-clockwise. Use this to drive the right elbow in an upwards swinging arc that delivers the strike under the opponent's chin. If the knees are quickly straightened just before contact, the lift in body weight adds momentum to the blow.

A rearwards travelling elbow strike can be used against the opponent who is standing immediately behind. Begin by taking up a left fighting stance and bringing the left foot back and behind the right. The length of the step will depend upon how far away the opponent is, so, before moving, look over your shoulder. If you step too far, you will bump into the opponent. If you step too little, you will be too far away for an effective strike. As you are stepping back, extend your left arm, fingers open. As your step is concluding, change your posture to a back stance and pull the extended left arm back as strongly as possible. As maximum weight descends upon the left foot, impact is made with the elbow. Provided you synchronize the impact with the last few millimetres of movement, this strike is extremely powerful.

The Knee

The knee is another powerful short-range weapon. It can be lifted directly into the target or describe a rising circular path. It is most commonly aimed at the face when the opponent has been doubled up by a blow to the mid-section. It is also used against the groin and the thighs. The most powerful straight knee kick is delivered with the back leg. Start from a fighting stance and swing the rear leg up and forwards in a rising arc. Arch your back and raise up onto the ball of your supporting foot as the knee finds its target. The toes of the striking leg point directly at the floor.

A turning knee strike also uses the back leg. The supporting leg swivels and, as the knee rises, the lower leg no longer points vertically downwards. The force of the strike depends upon the speed with which the kicking leg is raised and the rate at which the body is swivelled. The turning knee strike is useful against the opponent who is not facing directly forwards.

The Shin

The shin is quite vulnerable to injury but it also makes a very potent weapon if the foot is turned slightly so that impact is taken on the side. It is well suited to attacks against the opponent's thigh and jaw. In both cases, a turning kick is used to deliver it. The instep (**figure 34**) is a potent weapon when used against the groin, side of the face and the jaw. The toes are curled down and the ankle made rigid on impact. Ideally, the ankle should be extended until the instep is in line with the shin.

The Foot

The ball of the foot is a very strong and versatile weapon (**figure 35**). Unlike the instep, it is well padded and can withstand the occasional impact into an elbow or knee. It is, however, difficult to form properly and·needs a great deal of practice to achieve. In a front kick, the instep must be fully extended so it is in a straight line with the shin. Then the toes must be raised so they are clear of the impact area. To practise the configuration for ball of foot kicks, stand facing a table and rest your fingertips on it. Raise up on the balls of your feet, lifting your heels as high as they will go.

If the beginner fails to pull back his toes, he may suffer injury on impact with a solid object. Alternatively, he may draw back his toes but not be able to extend the instep so his kick is made with the sole and not the ball of the foot. This is wasteful of impact force and turns the technique into a shove. The sole of the foot is often used intentionally in a variety of front kick, to push the opponent back.

The outer edge of the foot is used in side snap kick. It is an efficient weapon because it concentrates force over a small area. Nevertheless, it is not so ·strong as the heel which is used in the technique known as side thrust kick. Extend your kicking leg out in front of you and turn the foot so the sole is facing the floor. Curl your ankle around so the foot is at right angles to the shin, then lift the toes (**figure 36**).

Figure 34 To use the instep, curl your toes downwards

Figure 35 Using the ball of the foot in front kick

Figure 36 The heel of the foot is used in side snap kick

Figure 37 The inner edge of the foot is used in crescent kick

Figure 38 In back kick, the heel leads the rest of the foot

The inner edge of the foot is used in the crescent kick. The foot is held vertically with the toes pointing upwards. The sole of the foot forms a scoop which can catch and lift the target. The foot is swung into the target which may be the leading fist, the side of the jaw (**figure 37**) or the back of the opponent's front foot.

In back kick, the heel leads the rest of the foot (**figure 38**). In reverse turning kick, the back of the heel is swung up and round into the side of the jaw or temple.

CHAPTER 6: BASIC TECHNIQUES OF TAEKWONDO

Once the theories of power generation have been understood and the student can form his hands and feet into effective weapons, it is time to incorporate the two into basic technique. Basic techniques are the individual punches, kicks and strikes upon which the martial art is built. It is impossible to launch an effective flurry of powerful techniques until the mechanism of delivering just one is mastered.

Each basic technique has a start and a finish and, during its execution, different factors must be considered. The instructor will describe the various points to look out for in stages and call for a single technique to be performed. This will be repeated many times during the lesson and, through assiduous practice, competence is built up.

Basic technique must be performed with a smooth action; all jerkiness and hesitation must be eliminated. The body is kept relaxed until the moment of impact, when it momentarily tenses to concentrate force. During the execution of a technique, body height must remain constant, with no tendency for the student to bob up and down. Non-involved parts of the body should be held firm but relaxed, so elbows and arms do not flap about. Every effort must be made to produce a clean line and fast delivery from the correct stance. The head is held high and attention is fixed to the front.

The Lunge Punch

The usual starting point for basic techniques is the lunge punch. This is a blow using forward motion of the body to generate momentum. It is at its most powerful when delivered from a forward stance since that stance is particularly suited to resisting recoil.

Commence in a left forward stance and extend your left fist, palm downwards and elbow straightened. Hold the right fist cocked and ready, palm upwards on the right side, at the level of the belt. The shoulders and hips are forwards facing. The front foot points directly forwards with the knee above it and bent forwards so it comes to lie over the instep. The rear foot is twisted as much to the front as possible and the knee is locked straight. The rear leg absorbs recoil so it is important not to bend it (**figure 39**).

The body must be held upright and the head turned

Figure 39 Lunge punch, commencing from left forward stance. The left arm is fully extended

Figure 41 Lunge punch. On impact strongly pull back the left arm

Figure 40 Lunge punch: keep the weight constant as you step through

to look to the front. Do not lean in any direction. On the command, step directly forward with the rear leg, letting it glide over the floor, instep resting lightly. The advancing leg passes the original front foot and continues on an equidistant path. It is important to keep the left leg bent during this move, otherwise the body will lift (**figure 40**).

Just as the advancing foot reaches its final position, several things happen at once. As the heel of the foot presses down on the floor, the left fist is withdrawn and the right simultaneously extended. The energy going into the withdrawal is also used to drive out the new punch. The orientation of the fists remains constant until the last instant, when both are rotated simultaneously. The right fist turns palm down and the left palm up. The left leg locks straight at the same time and the punch is driven into the target (**figure 41**).

There are a number of common mistakes to be avoided when practising this technique. The first concerns the leading fist. Many people withdraw the fist too early and without synchronizing it with the advancing punch. Others leave the fist out well enough, but allow it to wave about as the body steps forward. The cocked fist should not be allowed to move off the hip and the shoulders should not be hunched. Preserve the stance's natural side step by not drawing the advancing foot inwards as it passes the supporting leg.

As the punch is delivered, do ensure that the various components work together. A premature punch made before the front foot has settled with weight on it will throw the body forwards, yet lose a great deal of power. Punching too late means that the momentum of advance is lost and the blow has only the power of the arms. The punch must be delivered to the centre of an imaginary opponent's chest and not to his shoulder. The punching shoulder must not lead, otherwise the stance becomes unstable and open to an unbalancing pull. Finally, as in all punches, ensure it travels direct to the target. Do not allow the punching elbow to stick out or energy will be lost in recoil.

Reverse Punch

Reverse punch is similar in many ways to lunge punch except that the opposite fist to the leading leg is advanced. While the punch can be delivered from any stance where there is a front leg, reverse punch is at its strongest when used from forward stance. To practise it, start in left forward stance and advance your right fist, the palm turned downwards. The left fist is held ready palm upwards on the belt. Make sure that the punch is directed slightly inwards. On the command, step forwards exactly as for lunge punch and withdraw/ punch as the final stance is about to be achieved.

Because the opposite fist is used, the hips must turn more to strike the centre of the imaginary target. The rotation of the hips is used in conjunction with the pull-back to add power to the punch. Consequently, the hips must turn before the punch is released.

Use of the hips in this technique raises a few additional problems to be avoided. If the stance is too wide, the hips must turn too much to take the punch to its central target. This causes instability and a tendency to lead too much with the shoulder of the punching arm. If the hips do not drive forwards and lock, the upper body is incapable of absorbing the recoil of a heavy blow and will twist away from the impact.

The Jab

The jab uses the hips and upper body to generate power. It is best practised from walking or fighting stance. Take a short step forwards holding the original guard and, as weight comes down on the advancing foot, twist the shoulder of the punching arm forwards and withdraw the guard to just in front of the chin. Punch with the new leading fist and withdraw it immediately to guard position. When practising this basic technique, do not let the elbow rise and do not lean in with your chin or unguarded face.

Figure 42 Begin front kick from fighting stance

Figure 43 The rear leg is brought forwards and up

Front Kick

Front kick is best practised initially from fighting stance (**figure 42**). The kick begins with a simultaneous move affecting the upper and lower body. As the rear leg is brought forwards and up, the guard is changed. The kicking leg is well bent and the shin vertical (**figure 43**). The sole of the foot is parallel to the floor and is driven into the target with the toes pulled back (**figure 44**). The foot actually travels directly into the target and there is no upswinging arc which causes it to swing past the target if it falls short.

As the kicking knee is raised, the supporting foot turns outwards, aligning the hips for maximum effective range. The lower foot is then driven into the target and afterwards withdrawn. During the delivery of the kick, body weight must be kept over the bent supporting leg so it can be withdrawn quickly. If body weight is allowed to move forwards, the kick cannot be quickly withdrawn and instead lands heavily.

The front kick is smooth and continuous in its execution, accelerating quickly clear through to impact. There must be no hesitation as the knee reaches correct height, and involvement of the lower leg is begun a fraction before this position is reached. As in the lunge

Figure 44 The ball of the foot is driven into the target with toes pulled back

punch, momentum must be efficiently harnessed and the accelerating of the kicking knee provides a great deal of energy that must not be wastefully dissipated.

Timing is very important and several things happen at once. The supporting leg begins to rotate as the kicking knee is rising. At the same time the guard is changed to free the hip from any resistance due to torsion in the spine. By means of this change of guard, the student will find himself correctly equipped for a forward landing. When changing the guard, the elbows must be kept to the sides of the body, so there is no flapping around. Novices often hunch the shoulders during the kick and this must be avoided. The shoulders play no part after the guard has changed. Once the kick has concluded, it must be withdrawn before it is set down. Under no circumstances should it just be slammed down.

Different kinds of front kick

Two varieties of front kick are delivered with the sole of the foot. The first is delivered from the back leg in exactly the same way as the orthodox front kick. The supporting leg swivels, the guard is changed and the knee raises to the launch position. Instead of snapping straight into the target, the heel is dropped and the foot is driven into the target in a thrusting shove (**figure 45**). If the range is correct, the foot will contact while the kicking knee is bent and a sudden straightening drives the opponent back.

Because of the way the kick is used, weight must be projected more forwards, otherwise the user will be knocked back off balance. Contact with the target gives stability and allows the kicking leg to be directly set down on the ball of the foot. The positioning of the set-down will determine the type and range of the follow-up technique. Thrusting front kick is used to line up an opponent for another technique such as turning kick.

If the opponent rushes in, the front foot can be lifted up and extended out to check his advance. This variety of front kick should be performed from fighting stance and weight thrown forward upon impact. If weight is retained fully over the supporting leg, the body can be driven backwards and off balance. The guard must be carefully maintained throughout.

In delivering any kick, it is always a good idea to practise some of the moves with a preceding scissors step. This sudden flurry of movement makes a good feint and can remedy small faults in distance. To practise scissors step, start in left fighting stance and jump into the air. While aloft, quickly change your feet over and land with the right foot forwards, then launch the kick to be practised. When making scissors step, do not

Figure 45 A variety of front kick using the sole of the foot to push an opponent back

Figure 46 Front kick can be used in conjunction with a jumping step forwards. Start from fighting stance

jump too high into the air – just enough to be able to change your feet over. Only practise the scissors step from a short stance, otherwise it will take too long.

Where the range is greater, front kick can be used in conjunction with a jumping step forwards. From right fighting stance (**figure 46**) skip forwards on the left leg and draw up the right ready to kick (**figure 47**). As you land on the ball of the foot drive the kick straight out, then retrieve and set it down (**figure 48**). Make sure you skip forwards rather than up and raise your knee while in the air and not on landing, otherwise considerable momentum will be wasted.

Turning Kick
Turning kick takes the foot in a flattening horizontal curve into the target. For maximum power, the kicking foot should begin slightly higher than the target and then drop down slightly into it. The power for this kick derives from the substantial hip-twist and consequent rotation of the supporting leg. From left fighting stance (**figure 49**, overleaf), raise the back foot and bring it forward. At the same time, start swivelling on the supporting leg. Bring the knee of the kicking leg quickly across the front of your body and lean back from it (**figure 50**, overleaf). This not only balances the kick, it

Figure 47 As you land on the ball of the foot, drive the kick straight out

Figure 48 Retrieve the front kick and set it down

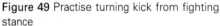

Figure 49 Practise turning kick from fighting stance

Figure 50 Bring the knee of the kicking leg quickly across the front of the body

also takes the body away from immediate counter-attack. When the knee has reached the correct height, lash out with the lower leg, connecting with either the ball of the foot or the instep (**figure 51**). Then you should pull the kick back and return to a more upright stance before setting the foot down.

The raising of the knee and the swivelling of the hips take place at the same time and there is a smooth acceleration throughout. The guard changes but otherwise remains firmly fixed to the sides. If the knee does not lift high enough, the kick will not deliver its full force into the target. The supporting leg must rotate until it is virtually facing the reverse way and the kicking hip is directly above the supporting hip. The back is arched outwards.

One step turning kick

One-step turning kick is performed in much the same way as one-step front kick. Jump forwards and raise the kicking leg while in the air (**figures 52, 53**). Land on the ball of your foot and immediately swivel your hips so the kicking hip rises up and above the supporting leg. Deliver the kick as the weight settles onto the supporting leg, so as not to waste energy (**figure 54**). Timing is of the essence and the body must turn

Figure 51 Drive out the lower leg

Figure 52 Start from a fighting stance

Figure 53 Jump forwards and raise the kicking leg while in the air

Figure 54 Deliver the kick immediately weight settles onto the supporting leg

while in flight so only the minimum need be done upon landing.

Side Kick

Side kick is best practised from a fighting stance (**figure 55**) by lifting the front leg and leaning back to maintain balance while removing the body from possible counter-attack (**figure 56**). The hips are rotated violently so the supporting leg comes to point backwards. The knee is straightened as the hips come to the end of their rotation and the foot driven out like a piston. Impact is made with the heel (**figure 57**).

The lifting of the front leg is very quick indeed. The driving of the kick outwards and the twist on the supporting leg are simultaneous. The kicking leg locks straight just as the supporting leg reaches the limit of swivel. The guard must be carefully aligned so the forward arm overlies the kicking leg and the other is folded across the chest. It is important to drive the edge of the foot out and not the sole of the foot. The head must be kept raised to preserve balance. After the kick has made contact, it is withdrawn and bent at the knee before being settled to the floor in a controlled manner.

It is also possible to side kick off the rear leg. Practise from a fighting stance (**figure 58**) and bring the rear leg up and forwards exactly as in a front kick. As the knee of the kicking foot reaches maximum height, the supporting leg rotates (**figure 59**) and simultaneously the kicking leg is driven out (**figure 60**). The back arches outwards and the guard is kept carefully aligned. Afterwards the kick is withdrawn and set down carefully (**figure 61**, overleaf). Novices tend not to turn the supporting leg enough in side thrust kick and there is a corresponding lack of penetration.

One-step side kick

One-step side kick is extremely fast and powerful. It is best performed from a high straddle stance (**figure 62**, overleaf). The back leg skips forward and the front rises with knee bent (**figure 63**, overleaf). The body turns away from the direction of flight and the kick extends just as the ball of the foot grazes the floor. As full weight settles, the heel is driven out and the knee locks straight (**figure 64**, overleaf). To counterbalance the forward rush of the kick, the body must lean well back, with the head held up and sighting over the top of the kicking leg. The arms must be kept from flying about.

Back Kick

Back kick uses a spinning motion to drive a thrust. Start from a left fighting stance (**figure 65**, overleaf), put

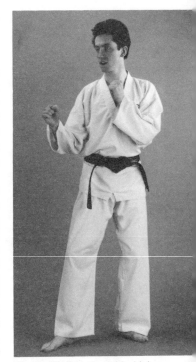

Figure 55 Practise side kick from fighting stance

Figure 56 Lift the front leg, leaning back to maintain balance. Maintain your guard

Figure 57 Drive the heel

Figure 58 (right) Side kick off the rear leg from fighting stance

Figure 59 The supporting leg rotates and the kicking knee rises

Figure 60 Twist your hip and lean back

Figure 61 The side kick is withdrawn and set down carefully

Figure 62 Practise one-step side kick from a high straddle stance

Figure 63 The back leg skips forward and the front one rises with knee bent

Figure 64 The kick is delivered immediately upon landing

weight on your leading left foot and twist your hips clockwise. This action must come from the hips themselves and not result from a dragging action by the shoulders. During the turn, the arms are kept to the sides and the right leg slides in an arc, preceding the turn. Weight is kept over the left leg so the right can be lifted up (**figure 66**) and driven back hard into the target. From being lifted up, the foot travels in a straight line, impacting with the heel (**figure 67**). The head rotates with the hip and the target is always kept in sight.

Beginners sometimes leave too much weight on the right foot with the result that it cannot move freely around with the hips. They may also turn with the shoulders and not the hips so the kick goes off centre. The turn itself is a sharp movement and the kick begins just as it is completing. There must be no delay during which the helpless back is presented to the opponent.

Figure 65 Practise back kick from a fighting stance

Figure 66 Swivel the hips and lift the kicking leg. Watch the target

Figure 67 The foot travels in a straight line, impacting with the heel

Axe Kick

Axe kick is a spectacular technique that uses gravity to enhance the force generated. From fighting stance the rear leg is swung forwards and up until the knee touches the shoulder (**figure 68**). The leg is kept completely straight and the arms are held ready at the sides. As the foot falls heel first, weight is moved forwards both to extend the range of the kick and to inject yet more power into it by adding body weight. The heel of the foot strikes the collarbone or centre of the opponent's head, though, for safety, the latter blow is often made with the sole of the foot.

Crescent Kick

Crescent kick is a long, sweeping technique that brushes incoming techniques to one side. From left fighting stance (**figure 69**) bring the rear leg up and forwards. The knee is not flexed so much as in previous kicks and the sole of the foot points towards the opponent (**figure 70**). The foot is lifted and swung across the front of the body in a flailing motion (**figure 71**) while the supporting leg rotates only minimally in comparison to the turning and side kicks.

At the end of its sweep, the kicking knee is bent sharply and the foot pulled in close to the body before being set down.

Figure 68 Axe kick: the rear leg is swung forwards and up

Reverse crescent kick

Reverse crescent kick uses the same body swivel as does back kick. From left fighting stance (**figure 72**), put weight on the ball of the front foot and rotate the hips clockwise. Turn fully until your back is towards the opponent and, as you reach this position, lift your right leg and hold it bent and well out from the body (**figure 73**). Continue the hip rotation and smoothly straighten the knee so the blocking outer edge of the foot sweeps past the front of the body with the outer edge leading (**figure 74**, overleaf).

The rotation continues still further and the knee once more flexes before the foot is returned to its starting position.

Reverse turning kick

Reverse turning kick uses exactly the same motion except that the position of the foot is altered. In reverse crescent kick, the toes point upwards, and in reverse turning kick they point to the side and the heel leads (**figure 75**, overleaf). Both kicks are powered by hip rotation; if this is inadequate or slow, the kick will be weak. The rotation must be maintained until the very end and the body returned to an upright position. If this is not done, the kick cannot be withdrawn promptly

Figure 69 Practise crescent kick from fighting stance

Figure 70 Raise the kicking leg

Figure 71 Drive the foot across the body

Figure 72 Practise reverse crescent kick from fighting stance

Figure 73 Twist your hips fully and raise the kicking leg

and the student is open to counter-attack. The head must turn sharply so the opponent is kept in view the whole time.

Flying Kicks (General)

The flying kicks are the next in a logical progression which begins with static kicks and then goes on to skipping kicks. The flying kick is a skipping kick in which the height component has been increased so the technique is actually delivered while the body is entirely airborne. Such kicks are powerful but they must be withdrawn before landing. Care must be taken to prevent elbows flying out during flight and the student must avoid staring at the ground. The propelling jump must reach a good height, otherwise there will be insufficient time to kick while both legs are clear. The jump must be made without too much preamble, otherwise the opponent will realize what you are about to do and counter it.

Flying front kick

The most basic of the flying kicks is flying front kick. Begin from a right fighting stance and step up and forwards with the left leg. Act as though you are stepping up onto an invisible high chair with that leg and then begin straightening it. Surge up off the right foot and bring the knee up against your chest. Then snap kick out with the right foot just as you are reaching the top of your rise. Make sure the kick begins before height is lost, otherwise the left leg will touch ground too early.

Flying turning kick

Flying turning kick uses a strong hip action while airborne. Start in right fighting stance (**figure 76**) and swing your left leg around and up as though you were performing a crescent kick. Jump up off the right leg as the left reaches halfway across the body. As you are rising, kick around with the right leg, allowing your hip to roll over the top of the left (**figure 77**). Strike with the instep.

Flying side kick

Flying side kick covers distance as well as height and impact is made with the heel. The supporting leg is fully retracted against the thigh of the kicking leg. This provides a reference point for determining how good the kick is. Start in left fighting stance (**figure 78**) and bring the back leg up and forwards as strongly as possible (**figure 79**). Straighten the left leg and throw the body into the air, then retract it fully. As the left leg leaves the ground, thrust out the right foot and allow your body to turn behind the kick (**figure 80**, overleaf).

Figure 74 Reverse crescent kick: continue the hip rotation and straighten the knee so the blocking outer edge of the foot sweeps past the front of the body with outer edge leading

Figure 75 In reverse turning kick the toes point to the side and the heel leads

Figure 76 Begin from a fighting stance

Figure 77 Jumping up, kick with the right leg

Figure 78 For flying side kick, start in fighting stance and . . .

Figure 79 . . . bring the back leg upwards and forwards whilst rising into the air

Figure 80 Straighten the left leg and twist

Figure 81 Begin from a fighting stance

Figure 82 Twist hips fully and lift the kicking leg

Figure 83 As the body turns, the kick begins to extend . . .

Figure 84 . . . pulling the body right around   **Figure 85** Flying reverse crescent kick

After the kick completes, withdraw it and land on the balls of the feet.

Flying back kick
  Flying back kick is difficult to execute correctly. Begin from left fighting stance (**figure 81**) with a combined hip rotation and jump off the left leg (**figure 82**). As the body turns, the right knee raises and flexes so that, just as the back is about to turn full on to the opponent (**figure 83**), the heel is driven out strongly in a straight line (**figure 84**). The straightening leg pulls the hips around fully and, during the pull back of the kicking leg, the body returns to face forwards once more.

Flying reverse crescent kick
  Flying reverse crescent kick uses much the same effect but body rotation during the jump is far more pronounced and is responsible for generating the kick's power. As in the normal reverse crescent kick, the knee is raised when the back is fully turned and the kick begins to develop as the rotation winds the body around to face forwards (**figure 85**). The kicking leg is retrieved before landing.

CHAPTER 7: TAEKWONDO BLOCKING TECHNIQUES

There are two ways of dealing with an incoming taekwondo kick or punch. The first is not to be there when it arrives and the second is to deflect it from its target. The first method is called evasion and the second blocking. Both play an important role in sparring techniques.

The kick or punch is aimed at a target, rather than just thrown haphazardly in the general direction of the opponent. For example, the opponent may try to punch you in the face by aiming that technique where your face is, or where he expects it to be when the punch lands. It therefore follows that if your face is somewhere else at that time you will not be hit. The timing required for a successful evasion is critical. If you move your face too early, the opponent will correct his aim accordingly. If you move your face too late . . .

Evasion
Evasion is undoubtedly the best form of defence against a strong technique. The weakest person is not disadvantaged because speed and timing, not strength, are what is required. When evading, it is very important that you move by only the smallest amount – that's all it takes to make the technique miss. A small movement leaves you close to the attacker when the latter is unable to defend himself adequately.

It is very difficult to do two things successfully at once and the man throwing a powerful punch is not able effectively to respond to a simultaneous attack. Therefore, if your attacker throws a straight kick at your groin or mid-section, move diagonally forward. The diagonal movement takes you a short distance to the side of the attack and closes the distance so you can safely counter. If you can counter before the attacker has managed to put his kicking leg down, he will be less able to avoid it.

The two mistakes to avoid in this practice technique are stepping too far to the side and leaving your counter too late. If you step too far away, you may exceed the range to use your fastest techniques and, if you leave your counter too late, he will land and regain his full potential for follow-up.

While evasions are undoubtedly the best way of dealing with the attack, they must nevertheless fit the circumstances. Ducking the head may be all right for avoiding a swinging punch at the head but it is not okay against an uppercut. Moving the head to one side may make the straight jab miss, but the curving hook will either follow the movement of the head or meet it at a slightly earlier stage. The evasion must therefore be properly selected to match the attack and, in the interests of safety, it is always recommended to block as well as evade.

The Block

A block interposes a part of your body between the blow and its target. Taekwondo blocks use the inner and outer parts of the forearm, the back and sides of the wrist, the palm of the hand, the edges of the hand, the back of the hand, the elbow, the knee and all parts of the foot.

For maximum effect, the block should either be applied before the attack it is meant to counter has built up full power or after the attack has missed and is slowing down. To provide the necessary body movement, blocks are best used in conjunction with an evasion technique. Only the strongest people can stand their ground and meet an attack strength for strength.

A turning kick to mid-section carries a lot of power and the leg is a weighty limb. It is not a good idea to remain stationary and try to block the kick using the forearm because the latter is likely to lose. If the turning kick is stopped before the lower leg is able to straighten, the opponent is unbalanced and prey to an effective counter. To try this, have your partner do a slow turning kick off his back leg. Carry your front guard well forward and, as the knee swings up and across, lean in and extend your open palm so it contacts the kick just below the knee. The effect of this is to throw the kicker off balance.

To practise the concept of effective distance, have the attacker step forwards and swing a downward hammer fist or knife hand to the centre of his head. Stand in a forward stance and lift your leading fist up and across your face, keeping it bent at the elbow, so the forearm finishes up by forming an inclined bar just above head height. The down-swinging head strike sooner or later intersects with this forearm bar and bruising can result. If, instead of standing your ground, you move forwards to meet the descending strike, you will block it at a lower point and it will be travelling correspondingly slower and with less energy – rather like the hub of a spinning wheel compared to the speed of the wheel rim.

As mentioned earlier, the block should never meet

the force of the blow full on. Body movement can reduce the force and a correct block can reduce it further. For example, stand in forward stance and have your partner aim a front kick to your mid-section. Stand your ground and swing your forward arm down in a lower block that meets the rising shin square on the forearm. The result of this is painful and frequently results in fractures. Now try it by swinging your blocking arm down in an arc, so, instead of the forearm directly meeting the upward rising shin, it strikes against the side of it. The forearm is now not trying to resist the movement of the shin but imparts a new impetus to it, causing the foot to be deflected rather than halted.

Deflection

The principle behind an effective block is that of deflection. Onrushing force is met with the minimum of response and rechannelled in a different direction. A rotating drum will throw off any attempts to poke it hard with a pole. In the same way, a combination of body movement and blocking technique throws off the attack.

Have your partner extend one arm fully and lock the elbow joint. Place the palm of your arm against their biceps and try to deflect the arm. Then repeat the movement, but this time put the palm of your hand against the wrist and push. The latter will cause greater deflection for the least effort because you are applying your force to the end of a lever. Therefore, wherever possible, apply the block to the end of a technique to gain the maximum deflection. There is a drawback to this and that is, unless you have taken the precaution of moving your body, you will be blocking the technique very close to its original target and not leaving yourself a large margin of error.

The closed fist makes quite an effective block, especially when used like a hammer against the attacking limb. It can be very painful for the opponent and, for this reason, is sometimes used as block and counter-attack all in one move. For example, there is a move in one of the patterns in which the opponent's punch is trapped by a double hammer fist block. The closer block takes the punch on the wrist and, simultaneously, the second hits the extended punching arm on the elbow, producing an agonizing over-straightening.

In like vein, a punch to the chest can be evaded by a short step back, while a combination palm and hammer fist block trap the blow, forming a hammer and the anvil on which the opponent's wrist is damaged. To try this, have your partner deliver a slowish punch and contact it with palm block close to your chest. At exactly the same time, slam right hammer fist into the other side of his wrist. When practising this, be sure to trace the path of the incoming punch with the movements of the two blocks. Don't just wipe them straight across the chest or they may arrive too early or too late to make contact.

Blocking with the wrist and hand

The back of the wrist makes an adequate block for a lower-powered strike. It must be coupled with a body movement and is really there to deflect rather meet the attack head on. The fingers are extended and the hand is bent back to form a hooking block that can pull down the attacking punch and then extend as palm heel. Bending the wrist forward provides yet another form of block suitable for close-range and lower-powered strikes. Bent wrist block is normally brought from waist height in an upwards direction.

The base of the palm is a potent block for slapping attacks off course. The fingers are curled in and the wrist bent back. The block is effective both as an impact and as a pressing block. In the latter guise, the palm can be brought upwards beneath a low-energy or slow-moving strike, lifting and extending it so it becomes unstable. The palm may also be used for a downwards pressing block with either a single or double hand. The incoming technique is merely pushed or slapped down to the floor. Knife block is used in a chopping or thrusting motion and is particularly effective against wrists and forearms. On the thumb side of the palm is reverse knife hand block. This is more difficult to target and is little used except as a back-up or low-energy block as a diversion.

The edges of the wrists are used during x-block. This interesting block is one of the few to meet a technique full on, relying on the energy-absorbing slide of one forearm over another to soak up the impact. The forearms are major blocking weapons and both thumb-side and little finger-side are used equally. The elbow is always deeply bent when these blocks are used, so they cover the maximum possible vertical as well as horizontal radius. The muscles which bring the arm from the outside of the body to the inside are stronger than those which take the arm from the centre of the body outwards and, for this reason, the block using the little finger-side of the forearm is more powerful.

Other ways of blocking

The elbow is an excellent close-range block used in conjunction with a body lean away from the attack. The forearm is held vertically downwards with the fist almost brushing the armpit. Incoming strikes are taken near the top of the elbow but there is a fair degree of latitude along the length of the forearm in which angled blows can be deflected. The knee is effective against another kick. Assume tiger stance and lift your front knee into the direction of the kick. This can cause extensive bruising to the opponent's shin and ball of the foot. The sole of the foot is used in crescent kick, to sweep a leading fist or kick to one side.

The x-block

To block a strike to the top of the head, use a head block or an x-block. Start in left forward stance and carry your hands in a completed head block position (**figure 86**). As your opponent swings his hammer fist down onto your head, move towards him and change into right forward stance, using the back leg as a prop. Block with the right arm by bringing it up close to your body with the fist leading (**figure 87**). As the fist passes across the front of your face, move it out and away from the body. At the conclusion of the move, twist your forearm violently so the little finger-side is uppermost (**figure 88**). Make sure your fist is higher than your elbow, so there is a sloping surface for the descending blow to meet and slide off.

Figure 86 Start in forward stance

To perform x-block, start in the same way and move into the strike. This time raise both arms up and across your body, so they intersect on a level with your throat, palms towards your face. From that point throw them up violently and rotate both forearms so the little fingers turn uppermost.

The x-block will also stop a straight punch to the face, as will an orthodox head block (**figure 89**). Straight punches to the face are best evaded by a lateral or straight back step. Knife block is another alternative which is particularly effective when used from a back or tiger stance. To practise knife block, begin in left back stance (**figure 90**) and step forwards into right back stance. As you step, bring your right arm back so the palm is near your left cheek. Extend your left hand forwards (**figure 91**) and, as you settle on the rear leg, withdraw your arm strongly. Use the effort involved in this to bring your right hand out and across in an arc before your face. Finish the block by abruptly turning it palm towards the opponent. At the same time it rotates, turn your left hand palm upwards and stop it in front of the breastbone (**figures 92, 93**, overleaf).

The knife block

The knife block can be strengthened by taking it past the left cheek and letting the left arm extend out to the side and behind (**figure 94**, overleaf). Then swing both arms in unison around to the front, rotating both palms

Figure 87 As you step through, bring the blocking arm close to the body

Figure 88 Twist the forearm so the little finger side is uppermost

Figure 89 Head block will deflect upwards a straight punch to the face

Figure 90 Knife block from back stance

Figure 91 As you step forwards, extend the non-blocking arm

Figure 92 Turn the right hand palm forwards

Figure 93 Knife block easily deflects a straight punch

Figure 94 Knife block can be strengthened by using both arms in unison

Figure 95 Swing both arms in the direction of the block

Figure 96 Inner block may be practised from forward stance

Figure 98 Twist the knuckles forward in the last instant

Figure 97 Extend the left fist palm down and take the right fist to the right temple

as the block is brought to a halt (**figure 95**). The swinging action of both arms makes the block more powerful and, for this reason, it is said to be 'augmented'.

The inner block

The inner block uses the little finger-side of the forearm in response to a straight punch or thrusting kick to the mid-section. To practise it, start from left forward stance (**figure 96**) and advance with your right leg into right forward stance. As you step, extend your left fist palm down and take your right fist up to your right temple, as though you were saluting with knuckles against your ear (**figure 97**). As you settle into the stance, withdraw your left fist as fast as you can and use this action to pull your right fist around and across your body. Twist the forearm knuckles forward in the last instant and this sudden rotation will provide a bonus in power (**figure 98**). At the time when the block contacts the attacking punch, ensure the top of your blocking fist is level with your shoulder. At the same time there should be a right-angle bend at the elbow and the fist should not move ahead of the elbow (**figure 99**). If these provisions are observed, the block will sweep the maximum area.

The outer block

The little finger-side of the forearm can also be used as an outer block that moves from the centre to the outside. This is practised exactly the same as the knife hand block, using a back stance (**figure 100**) and stepping through. Cross the arms over, with one leading and the other pulled back across the side of the jaw (**figure 101**). Use the pull-back of the leading arm to power the blocking arm out and across the body (**figures 102, 103**).

Parallel vertical forearms are used as a powerful checking block against turning kicks. The upper body must turn to face the oncoming kick. This block uses no deflection and is not recommended for slightly built students.

A second double block uses the little finger-side of the forearms. It begins like a mid-section x-block, with the forearms crossing palm up in front of the chest. They then move outwards and away from each other, the fists closing and rotating palms down.

Outer block uses a motion like a windscreen wiper to scoop an attack to one side. Stand in left back stance

Figure 100 Outer block from back stance

Figure 101 Step up with the back leg and extend the non-blocking arm

Figure 99 There should be a right-angle bend at the elbow and the fist should not lead the technique at any stage

Figure 102 Use pull-back to power the block

Figure 103 Outer block from back stance is similar to knife block

and assume the blocking position, with left arm well bent and the blocking fist level with your shoulder (**figure 104**). Step forwards and trail your right arm down and across the front of your belt. Extend the left well forwards and use this to power the block (**figure 105**, overleaf). As you settle into the new back stance, pull the left arm back and swing up the right across the body. Keep your blocking elbow well bent and stop the action when your blocking arm is level with the shoulder (**figure 106**, overleaf). Any movement beyond this point is wasteful and slows the possibility of a counter-attack. Take care to keep the fist and elbow in one straight line and do not let either lead in the blocking movement (**figure 107**, overleaf).

Blocking kicks

Kicks to the mid-section and groin are dealt with either by x-block or by using a form of hammer block that sweeps in an arc down and across the lower part of the body. Start in left forward stance (**figure 108**, overleaf) and advance with the right leg into right forward stance. As you reach the in-between point in the step, bring your right arm up and across the front of your neck. Raise the left arm and bring it up and forwards, away from the body (**figure 109**, overleaf). As you settle into the new forward stance, strongly pull back your left arm and swing the right down and across, so it knocks the incoming kick out to the side. Stop the block when the fist is just to the right of the front knee;

Figure 104 Orthodox outer block has the blocking knuckles facing downwards

Figure 105 Extend the non-blocking arm

Figure 106 Pull back the non-blocking arm

Figure 107 Take care to keep the fist and elbow in one straight line and do not let either lead

Figure 108 Lower block practice begins from forward stance

Figure 109 As you reach the in-between point in the step, bring the blocking arm up and across the front of the neck

Figure 110 Stop the block when the fist is to the outside of the front knee

any further is unnecessary (**figure 110**).

The forearm can also be used in an effective scooping block that curls under a mid-section kick and draws it out. Practise by standing in left fighting stance and facing your opponent, who is also in left stance. He aims a front kick from his right leg and you move your body to the left, out of direct line of attack. As the kick approaches, swivel your hips fully so you turn almost completely parallel to it. At the same time, bring your left forearm up in a hooking movement that catches the kick at the lower part of the calf and raises and extends it. If the opponent stands in right stance, then to use the above block would open you to counter-attack, since you would be moving into the range of his left punch. Therefore, as the kick approaches, swiftly transfer weight and change to a left tiger stance, pulling your front foot back as you do. Block down and around, catching the opponent's heel in an over-hand grasp.

CHAPTER 8: TAEKWONDO COMBINATION TECHNIQUES

Combination techniques are series of basic techniques linked together into a continuous flow. The basic technique, consisting as it does of individual punches or kicks, can form the basis for a valid attack or defence, providing that factors such as timing and distance work in its favour. However, relying on one technique does have its drawbacks in that, if it misses, the athlete is left high and dry until he can produce a second. It is always better to attack an opening strongly with one technique, but having the possibility of another immediately to hand if it fails. This is the principle of combination techniques.

Combination techniques allow the taekwondo athlete to maintain a constant pressure of effective techniques against an opponent. If the basic techniques are skilfully linked, they produce a bewildering variety of strong attacks from varying angles and different directions, the effect of which is substantially to increase the possibility of a scoring hit.

Developing Combination techniques
To develop combination techniques, the format of some basic techniques must be altered slightly. The basic lunge and reverse punch are not withdrawn but remain extended until the next step. This does not lend itself to a rapid follow-up technique and so the method of doing them must be modified to withdraw the punch after it has landed or missed. This does not mean the technique is any less powerful; it is merely less static.

Usage of one technique may predispose the body to a certain follow-up. A good example is seen in a fairly basic combination technique which combines a mid-section reverse punch with a turning kick to the head. As the reverse punch is made, the punching hip turns square on to the opponent and weight is transferred forwards onto the leading leg. This combination of weight transfer and hip rotation takes weight off the rear leg, which is then free to rise. As the punching fist is withdrawn, the rear foot can begin rising into a turning kick aimed at the side of the opponent's jaw.

If the reverse punch to the mid-section is valid and not merely a feint, the opponent will have to respond and bring his leading hand down to block it. It will take a measurable time for the opponent to retrieve the block and return to a normal ready guard and, if the turning kick arrives during this in-between time, it has a good chance of success. Aiming at different targets with successive techniques taxes the opponent's concentration and ability and, if the combination technique is effectively sustained for long enough, there is a distinct possibility of scoring.

To develop and reach a fair degree of competence in a selection of combination techniques takes both time and ingenuity. They are extremely personal training forms and the student should be encouraged to develop his own. When doing so, he should consider a number of salient points. The first is that the individual techniques comprising the sequence should quickly follow each other, otherwise the opponent will treat them as a series of separate basic techniques rather than a fusillade of attacks.

Secondly, each technique must be a possible end in itself. This means that every component attack in a combination sequence must stand a chance of scoring and not just be a meaningless gesture that the opponent can profitably ignore. Feints using a simulated punch or kick have only a limited value and, wherever possible, they should be replaced by a potentially scoring technique which in any case serves the same purpose.

Using Combination Techniques Effectively

It is quite a different thing to use changes of stance or attitude as feints. The purpose of a feint is to divert the opponent's attention by means of a move which misleads him. To divert the opponent, the feint must appear to be a genuine and threatening move which requires a response. For example, a sudden move towards the opponent will cause him either to retreat or to stand his ground and get ready to make a response for something which does not materialize. Therefore a comprehensive repertoire of taekwondo combination technique must include sudden changes of stance and direction and, like the techniques themselves, these shifts must relate logically to follow-up moves.

Practising combinations

Combination techniques are not only useful for attack, they are a mainstay of defence. It is not enough merely to block the opponent's attack, a counter-attacking technique must be employed. For this to be effective, it must follow the block by the shortest possible interval. For example, if the opponent side kicks to mid-section and you block it with inner block, there will be a short time during which the attacker retrieves

the spent kick before resuming the attack. The combination technique of block and counter-punch must be
so timed as to catch the opponent in this in between
time, before he is ready for his next attack. Therefore
combination techniques must employ an element of
timing which reflects the practical application of each
move.

In view of their dual role for attack or defence, it must
be possible to perform them while advancing, while
retreating or while merely standing still. The resolute
attacker may well drive his opponent back and it will be
necessary to slow his onrush with effective and mobile
counters. Space may be seriously limited, in which case
he must simply stand his ground. Where the opponent
retreats, the combination technique must allow for an
advancing series of moves carried forward at such a
rate as to out-pace his retreat.

Combination techniques are practised both in pair-
form and alone. In the former case, they are more
correctly termed 'pre-arranged sparring'. When training
alone, it is customary to practise using a mirror to look
for errors in guard or openings where the opponent
may counter-attack. Mirror practice is very useful for
rehearsing the skilled movements needed to link techniques but it will be necessary to supplement it with
impact work done against the bag or target mitts.

In the more elaborate combination techniques, the
body spins around and it is easy to lose balance. Where
this happens, it is due mainly to simple lack of practice.
If, during a combination technique, balance is lost, then
effectiveness of the combination is lost also and the
individual attacking moves become disorganized,
scrappy and, above all, prey to a counter-attack. If
balance is lost, the combination must be halted in order
to allow the athlete to recover his equilibrium.

To reduce the possibility of effective counter-attacks
scoring, the student must maintain his guard throughout
any combination. When throwing a right reverse punch,
for example, the left hand must guard the face; when
using a turning kick, the arms must be kept close to the
body from where they can block effectively. During
moves where the body turns completely around, the
head must turn ahead to check that the athlete is not
moving into a counter-attack. Allied to this must be the
ability to halt the combination at any point, if the need
arises. Inexperienced people tend to throw themselves
into a combination without pausing to see the effect of
each separate technique before going on to the next.

Body positioning is very important too and weight
must always be kept in the balance and not committed
one way or another. Less experienced athletes will tend
to throw their weight forward during a combination

technique, causing kicks to slap down after use instead of being carefully placed. This slows the sequencing because corrections must constantly be made to recover balance or limbs that have ended up in the wrong place. During kicks, the upper body must be kept relaxed and the arms held in an effective guard. Constant body height must be maintained throughout the combination, except during flying kicks. The whole essence of combination technique is that of one move complementing (and not detracting from) another.

The force of each technique must be sharply contained if they are not to blur into each other. When this happens, individual technique definition is lost and scoring points becomes less likely.

Simple Combination Techniques

The combination technique consists of a series of punches, a series of kicks or a combination of the two. The simplest begin with two techniques and elaborate from there. Perhaps the most elementary combination is the snap punch/reverse punch sequence used to open a great many attacks. Begin from left fighting stance by transferring weight onto your front leg and throwing a quick left jab to mid-section. Be sure to turn your hip behind the jab, so it picks up a fair degree of power. Pull it back as quickly as it went out and use this action to power a mid-section reverse punch off the right hand. In this second punch, the back leg drives the body forwards, making the punch that much more powerful. The hips also turn square on, lending further penetration to the punch. The reverse punch must be quickly drawn back after use.

The effectiveness of this simple combination technique depends upon the small interval between the two powerful punches. The pull-back of the snap punch provides impetus for the second, so it is important not to isolate one from the other. To make the technique a little more complicated, it can begin with a scissors step feint that quickly changes the stance before the jab. Start in right stance, then scissors step so your left leg comes forward and, in the same instant that it lands, snap out the left jab.

Variations of the Combination Techniques

A variation of the combination interposes a step between two jabs and makes it more suitable for running down a retreating opponent. Start in right stance and scissors step to left. As you land, snap out left snap punch, then, as you withdraw it, step forwards a short distance only into right fighting stance. As your weight comes down on the right foot, snap out a right jab. Conclude the sequence with a left reverse punch.

The scissors step covers no ground but serves to confuse the opponent. The single step does cover ground but it must be hidden in the pull-back of the first jab. The second jab comes the instant the right foot touches down and so only a short step should be taken to minimize delay. The opponent must see two advancing punches and not a one-pause-two, followed by reverse punch.

The jab makes a very good opening for any combination because it is performed with the fist closest to the opponent, involves the least body movement, is fast and unsettling.

It is also possible to use an advancing simple combination technique which combines a fast forward or diagonal step with a powerful reverse punch. This again is ideal for driving the opponent back. Start in left stance and step quickly with the right foot, keeping your left fist well forward. As weight comes down on your right foot, drive out the left fist in a reverse punch.

A combination technique can also consist of kicks, the most simple being a front kick followed by a turning kick. To practise this, stand in a fighting stance (**figure 111**) and front kick off the rear leg with or without a preliminary scissors step (**figure 112**). Ensure that you keep your guard and pull the toes back. Withdraw the kick and drop it in front of the supporting leg (**figure 113**). Transfer weight across and onto the front leg, lifting up the back one, swivelling on the new supporting leg (**figure 114**) and delivering a turning kick with the toes pointing (**figure 115**).

To do this technique properly requires a positive pull-back of the front kick and careful positioning as it lands. If you drop the spent front kick close to the supporting leg, the turning kick will not be advanced too much. If, on the other hand, you land well forwards after the first kick, the second will move you forward. Use careful placement of the landing foot to control the distance covered in the combination. In similar vein, practise using a front kick combined with a side thrusting kick off the rear leg.

Of more practical use is a front thrust kick off the rear leg which drives the opponent back, lining him up for an axe kick. Front kick is very suitable for starting off a combination because it is fast and does not use a restrictive launching stance which can seriously limit the choice of follow-ups. Compare this with a reverse turning kick which is vulnerable to counter-attack unless a diverting technique is used first.

A turning kick and back kick make an interesting combination to practise with because, not only is there a complete body rotation, but the techniques change in character from a circular kick to a straight thrusting

Figure 111 Combinations are best practised from fighting stance

Figure 112 Front kick off the rear leg

Figure 113 Withdraw the kick and drop it in front of the supporting leg

Figure 114 Lift the back leg, swivelling on the new supporting leg . . .

Figure 115 . . . and deliver a turning kick with toes pointing

kick. From left fighting stance, kick off the rear foot and allow the supporting leg to swivel fully. Focus the turning kick and drop it quickly to the floor in line with the supporting leg. Twist the hips further in the same direction and back kick strongly with the right leg, bringing the weight backwards and over the supporting leg as you do. Impact with the heel to the opponent's mid-section and withdraw the foot while simultaneously continuing the rotation of the body until you are forward facing once more. When practising this combination, make sure you look over your shoulder during back kick so that you do not turn into a strong counter-attack.

The most successful combinations are those which combine the speed of hand techniques with the range and power of foot techniques. The simplest is the reverse punch and turning kick combination previously mentioned. In a combat situation, the fighter may or may not scissors step first, but he will lead with a short, fast jab off the leading fist. Immediately afterwards he reverse punches, throwing his weight forward and allowing the rear foot to rise. As this second punch is withdrawing, so the turning kick is delivered to the side of the opponent's jaw.

Advanced Combination Techniques
A slightly more difficult version of this uses a jab to divert the opponent, followed by back kick. Start in right fighting stance (**figure 116**) and snap punch off the front fist (**figure 117**). Then twist your hips to the left and turn your back towards the target, keeping your elbows close to the body (**figure 118**). Put weight over the right leg and back kick strongly with your left foot (**figure 119**). Continue turning your body and withdraw the kicking foot, setting it down carefully and resuming a new fighting stance.

A variation of this technique uses body rotation in the opposite direction. From left stance (**figure 120**), snap punch off the front hand (**figure 121**), then reverse punch with right fist (**figure 122**, overleaf). Pull back the reverse punch as strongly as possible and rotate your hips in the opposite direction to the punch (**figure 123**, overleaf). Support your weight on the left leg and allow the right foot to lift, driving it back into the target for a straight thrust kick (**figure 124**, overleaf).

A more complicated sequence starts from left fighting stance (**figure 125**, overleaf) with leading fist jab (**figure 126**, overleaf). The hips are then rotated in the opposite direction until the back is facing the opponent. Make sure you look over your shoulder at this point, to ensure that the coast is clear (**figure 127**, overleaf). Drop your weight onto the left leg and continue to rotate your

Figure 116 From fighting stance . . .

Figure 117 . . . snap-punch off the front fist

Figure 119 Put the weight over the back leg and back-kick strongly

Figure 118 and turn your back to the target

Figure 120 From fighting stance . . .

Figure 121 . . . snap-punch off front hand

Figure 122 Then reverse punch

Figure 123 Rotate in the opposite direction . . .

Figure 124 . . . and deliver back kick to mid-section

Figure 125 From left fighting stance . . .

Figure 126 . . . jab with the front fist

Figure 127 Then twist your hips right around

Figure 128 As your hips rotate, deliver a reverse crescent kick

body back around to the front. On the way, pick up your right foot and bring it up and across in a reverse crescent kick (**figure 128**). Allow the kick to travel right across the front of your body before dropping it to the floor and transferring weight over it. Continue hip rotation and lift your left foot into a turning kick to mid-section (**figure 129**, overleaf). Bring the kick back, placing the foot down carefully in front and conclude the sequence with a reverse punch (**figure 130**, overleaf).

Circular kicking techniques are both extremely powerful and difficult to block. They form the basis for several of the more advanced combinations used during competition taekwondo. One of the most popular uses a jab from the front fist followed by a reverse punch. The rear foot then rises into a turning kick and is not pulled back, carrying on over and around until it sets down near the supporting leg. Weight is then transferred onto it as the body continues to rotate in the same direction and the other leg lifts off to deliver reverse turning kick. Make sure you occasionally alter the direction of rotation between successive turning kicks to confuse your opponent's guard and increase the likelihood of a score.

Figure 129 Use continuing hip rotation to power a turning kick to mid-section

Figure 130 Retrieve the kick and conclude with a reverse punch

CHAPTER 9: TAEKWONDO PATTERNS

Patterns, or 'forms' as they are also known, are sequences of combination techniques performed in a set order. They are representations of combat with imaginary multiple attacks converging from different directions. There are many different types of pattern, each containing a different mixture of techniques.

It is quite obvious that the Korean patterns practised in taekwondo are a recent development though they may well claim to have their earliest roots in traditional martial art.

What a Pattern is for
The pattern is essentially a training aid, allowing the usage of potentially dangerous techniques in perfect safety since the opponent exists only in the mind of the person practising. The various patterns have different levels of complexity and can be conveniently linked to the grading syllabus. They serve as the best possible means of competence assessment since all of taekwondo's major techniques are included therein in a form which lends itself to easy examination.

Repetition is one of the best ways of learning techniques and the pattern presents an unparalleled opportunity to repeat complex movements until their performance becomes almost automatic. The ability to perform a complex series of fighting techniques without conscious thought as to 'what goes where' is a cornerstone of effective fighting. Therefore the pattern has a very real part to play in the development of taekwondo as an effective combat system.

Whereas combination technique consists basically of linear movement, the pattern incorporates movement in all directions. An opponent is visualized and responded to by a combination of defensive and offensive moves before attention is directed elsewhere and the sequence repeated in another direction. The pattern encapsulates all the underlying theories and practices of taekwondo so, to understand the system, it is necessary to understand the patterns.

Pattern Training and Practising
To the novice, pattern training is a meaningless series of techniques to be learned before the next grading examination can be taken. The novice is so taken up

with remembering the order in which the moves come that he is totally preoccupied. It is only once the moves have been learned and do not have to be consciously thought of that the student can introduce understanding and deeper feelings for the moves.

This knowledge is reflected in the way students tackle pattern practice. The novice treats the pattern as a race, speeding through it from beginning to end, blurring techniques into one another and losing focus and definition. The advanced student performs the pattern at a more sensible speed and cadence, completing each technique clearly and with considerable force before going on to the next.

When practising the pattern, it is important to compose the mind and calm the breathing. The pattern starts and finishes on one spot and the technical accuracy of the techniques used will be reflected in any deviation found at the finish. Breathing has to be coordinated with the rhythm of the movements, so it is forcefully expelled during violent techniques. The movements must be fluid and relaxed, except momentarily when the technique's power is concentrated to a peak. The speed of the pattern must be in accord with the meanings of the techniques and there must be perfect balance, with no staggering in stance or faltering in the execution of the techniques.

The Various Patterns
The following are some of the forms practised in taekwondo.

Choi-yong is named after General Choi Yong, a civil and military leader of the fourteenth-century Koryo Dynasty. The pattern has forty-six movements.

Chon-ji deals with the roles of heaven and earth in the beginning of mankind. It is a pattern of nineteen moves, divided into two parts, one representing 'heaven' and the other 'earth'.

Choong-jang was the pseudonym of General Kim Duk Ryang who lived in the fifteenth century (Yi Dynasty). The pattern is comprised of fifty-two movements.

Choong-moo is named after the Korean admiral Yi Sun-Sin who is claimed to have invented the first armoured warship in AD 1592. The pattern consists of thirty movements.

Dan-gun is named after Dangoon, the legendary founder of Korea. The pattern bearing his name consists of twenty-one movements.

Do-san honours the Korean patriot Ahn Chang Ho who opposed the Japanese domination of his homeland. The pattern has twenty-four movements.

Eui-am is the pseudonym of the patriot Son Byong

Hi and consists of forty-five movements.

Ge-Baek is named after the seventh-century general of that name and consists of forty-four movements.

Hansoo is named after the principle of water. It is a pattern consisting of twenty-seven moves in six different directions. Water flows everywhere and can defeat the hardest substance by flowing around, rather than by opposing, it.

Hwa-rang is named after the elite young warriors of the Silla Dynasty who were responsible for unifying Korea. The pattern has twenty-nine movements.

Ilyo is the state of spiritual enlightenment sought by the serious student of taekwondo. It only comes about when the practitioner has gone beyond the realms of simple technique, so his mind is uncluttered by thoughts of how he will deal with an attack, or what technique is to be preferred above another. The taekwondo student who has obtained ilyo has 'forgotten' all he has learned. It has gone from his conscious mind where it only inhibits his natural reactions. Therefore this pattern of twenty-four moves symbolizes the attainment of the clear and far-seeing mind.

Jitae uses the principle of power from one's roots, since it is based upon the Oriental concept of the earth as the producer and receiver of all things. The pattern consists of twenty-eight moves.

Joong-gun honours the patriot An Joong Gun who was responsible for assassinating the first Japanese Governor-General of occupied Korea. The pattern comprises thirty-two moves.

Keumgang describes the concept of the 'mind like a diamond' that is tough, resolute and self-sufficient. This is a well-known Zen Buddhist principle dating back to the days of the Shaolin Temple. The diamond is the hardest known substance and it is also very beautiful. For the latter reason, the name 'Keumgang-san' has been given to one of Korea's most beautiful mountains. The form contains twenty-seven movements, to be performed with a strong and calm mind.

Ko-dang is a pseudonym for the patriot Cho Man Sik. The pattern named after him is made up of thirty-nine moves.

Koryo is named after the Korean dynasty of that name (AD 918–1392), founded when the three previously independent kingdoms which made up what is now Korea amalgamated into one. The Koryo Dynasty was characterized by unity, strength and national resolve. Korea was, at that time, a land under seige, and it was only through this great national strength that the dynasty was able to prevail against overwhelming odds. Consequently, the Koryo pattern is performed strongly and with obvious determination to inject as much meaning and power into its moves as possible. The pattern consists of thirty moves.

Kwang-gae was the nineteenth-century King of the Koguryo Dynasty, famous for winning back occupied lands belonging to Korea. The pattern named after him consists of thirty-nine moves. It begins with 'a look to heaven'.

Moon-moo was the thirtieth King of the Silla Dynasty, crowned in AD 661. The pattern named after him consists of sixty-one moves.

The *Palgwe* are a series of eight training patterns based upon the *pa kua* (eight trigrams) of the *I'Ching*, which tries to explain the relationship of all things within the universe. Practice of the palgwes has now been largely superseded by the taegeuks. The principles within the two sets of patterns are essentially the same; that of steadfast opposition as opposed to yielding compliance, that of penetrating hardness counterbalanced by yielding softness.

Po-eun is named after the fifteenth-century poet Chong Mong-chu. The pattern contains thirty-six movements.

Pyongwon is the flat plain upon which the majority of people live. It provides the food of the nation and possesses a vastness which imbues it with grandeur. The form of that name tries to express the expanse of the plain through extended lateral movements.

Sam-il honours the foundation of the independence movement in Korea during 1919. Its thirty-three movements commemorate the patriots who founded the movement.

Se-jong is named after King Se-Jong who devised the Korean alphabet in AD 1443. The pattern named after him is comprised of twenty-four movements – one for each letter of the Korean alphabet.

Sipjin pattern is based upon the concept of orderly development and stability. It consists of thirty-one moves. An interesting combination occurs in one of them in which a front kick is followed by an augmented back fist delivered from a crossed-leg stance.

So-san is the pseudonym of the warrior monk Choi Hyung Un. The pattern consists of seventy-two movements – said to represent his age when he organized a counter-terrorist group to deal with pirates. This is the longest of the taekwondo patterns.

Taebaek is the legendary site where Korea was first founded by Dangoon. Taebaek is now known as Mount Baeckdoo, the tallest mountain in Korea. The form has twenty-six movements.

The *taegeuks* are training patterns upon which a competence in taekwondo is built. They embody all the principles of taekwondo. The origin of the title lies in the Chinese Book of Changes, the I'Ching, and it seeks to express a concept of completeness – embodying all things within its practice. Therefore, the first taegeuk, *keongwe*, symbolizes the beginning, the source of all things to come. The second expresses the principles of joyfulness (*tae*) as a clear and relaxed mind, full of positive thoughts. Taegeuk number three espouses the principle of *ri*, or 'fire'. This expresses itself as keenness and enthusiasm in practice. The principle of *jin*, or 'thunder', underlies the practice of the fourth. This is expressed as bravery and steadfastness, both necessary traits for the martial artist.

The fifth taegeuk is based upon the principle of *seon*, the 'wind', which may suddenly change direction or force without warning. Therefore the principle of the pattern is one of contrasts; the gentle movements contrasting with the violent. Taegeuk number six takes as its motif the formlessness of water (*gam*), flowing around and absorbing all things. The stone dropped into a pool sinks through it without resistance, leaving the water untroubled. The seventh taegeuk is founded upon the principle of *gan*, the 'immovable mountain'. This pattern reflects the need to combine movement and non-movement in response to an attack. Taegeuk number eight follows the concept of *gon*, the 'earth' from which all new things come. It reviews the fundamental issues contained in the previous seven taegeuks and provides a platform from which the more advanced patterns can be studied.

Toi-gye is the pseudonym of the neo-Confucianist scholar Yi Hwang. The pattern comprises thirty-seven movements.

Tong-il's fifty-six movements are dedicated to the wish for a united Korea.

Ul-ji honours the General Ul-ji Mun Duk who repulsed a Chinese force of more than one million soldiers in the seventh century. The pattern consists of forty-two movements.

Won-hyo is the Buddhist monk who reputedly introduced Zen Buddhism to Korea in the late seventh century. The form contains twenty-eight movements.

Yon-ge is named after a famous general of the Koguryo Dynasty who, in the middle seventh century, drove out a large Chinese occupying force. The pattern is made up of forty-nine movements.

Yoo-sin is dedicated to the seventh-century Korean military leader who unified the three Korean kingdoms. The pattern named after him has sixty-eight moves.

Yul-kok is the pseudonym of the great sixteenth-century Confucian scholar Yi I. The pattern named after him consists of thirty-eight moves.

CHAPTER 10: PRE-ARRANGED SPARRING IN TAEKWONDO

Pre-arranged sparring is a category of pair-form training in which one partner attacks and the other defends, according to a predetermined routine. Various degrees of freedom can be introduced as the participants become more skilled, but only by mutual agreement and fore-knowledge. Regardless of the amount of flexibility allowed, pre-arranged sparring always contains some limitation on the attack or defence and it is that which distinguishes it from free sparring.

Pre-arranged sparring forms a natural bridge between the pattern and free sparring. The pattern uses full power techniques which could be dangerous if applied to another person in an uncontrolled manner, but its practice is solitary and free from the sound and fury of actual combat. Furthermore, the results of its techniques can only be seen in the mind. Free sparring, on the other hand, presents the fighter with a real-life opponent capable of inflicting injury if he is not countered effectively. Pre-arranged sparring allows dangerous techniques, otherwise banned from free sparring, to be used in a safe situation where their deployment can be actually seen and not just visualized.

The Purpose of Pre-arranged Sparring
Practised correctly, pre-arranged sparring tests the attacker's power, resolve and speed and the defender's distance, timing and technical ability. It can be extremely strenuous and applied with such vigour that, if the defender fails to make the correct move, he can fall foul of the attack, predetermined or not.

Pre-arranged sparring is most commonly used to test the defender's abilities though its usage need not be restricted solely to that. It can also provide both partners with a means of assessing the value of their free sparring techniques. When used in this way, the defensive response can become merely a make-safe while the attack receives the greater attention.

Practising Pre-arranged Sparring
The first thing to do before commencing practice is to decide who will play the roles of attacker and defender and for how many repetitions those roles will be held

before changing. Confusion over role can result in injuries so it must be clarified at the outset. It is customary to assume each role alternately, taking one turn each as attacker and defender. In three-step sparring, this method is used in class lines where it is economical of space. In private rather than class practice, each role can be held for three or more repetitions before exchanging. By this means, mistakes can be corrected while they are still fresh in the mind.

The attacker must always inject as much realism into the attack as possible. He will start off slowly, especially if the sequence is newly learned, and gradually increase the pace as expertise grows. The uncooperative attacker can completely demoralize the defender by hurrying the pace of training, so the latter never has a chance to perfect the intricacies of techniques in his rush to simply avoid the attack. At the other extreme, the attacker must not be too accommodating, never providing more than slow, easy attacks which can be countered without effort. He must always test the defender's abilities if the latter is to improve.

The attack may be only a single punch or kick but, once the defender has achieved competence in his defence, it must be applied as though for real. By this means the defender will be able to experience the accuracy, speed and determination behind a genuine attack and learn to deal with it by the correct application of skill. A weak attack will lack this realism and, although the defender may learn to counter it, he will be learning something of limited use only. Pre-arranged sparring is the ideal platform to develop a strong spirit in safety and realism. It should not be regarded as a mere exercise in technique.

In furtherance of this aim, no special accommodations must be made which defeat the object of the training. The attacker who knows his kick is to be deflected to the left may decide to angle it that way. In consequence, the defence is altered slightly and the deflection never learned properly. Conversely, because the sequence is pre-arranged, the attacker will know that the defender is going to move in a particular way. If he alters his attack to take this into account, the value of the sequence is again lost. The attacker must always behave as though he did not know what to expect beyond the success of his attack.

In a similar way, the defender must behave as though each attack is entirely unexpected. This is very difficult to achieve and there will be a tendency for him to begin the set defence well before the technique would have been recognized in actual combat.

This occurrence is often seen during pre-arranged sparring. The attacker or defender forgets the technique and the defence made with such mechanical competence bears no relationship to the attack used. To achieve realism, the partners must work in unison, with correct pauses between strong individual attacks. Some people practise like automatons, jerking back and fore, going through the movements but never practising the technique properly. Each attack must be performed as though it was for the first time and the maximum effort employed by both attacker and defender.

When beginning practice, the partners face each other and perform a formal bow, then one or both will adopt a fighting or basic stance. After adopting starting stance, the attacker must settle himself down and summon the necessary reserves of power and aggression and, when ready, he launches forwards and delivers the attack. The defender waits for the attacking movement to begin, correctly identifies and then responds to it. At the conclusion of the technique, the defender administers the *coup de grâce* and there is a slight pause before both withdraw warily to their starting positions.

The withdrawal is a tactical move, its purpose being to remove the combatants from effective striking distance of each other. Although an opponent may appear beaten, in actuality he may not be and, by stepping forward with guard down, you may very well walk into a further attack. In free sparring, sometimes only one of the fighters hears the referee's command to stop and, if he steps forward to withdraw, he could very easily move into a punch or kick. After each withdrawal, the partners do not need to come to attention and bow. Formal salutation is restricted to the beginning and end of pre-arranged sparring.

Before commencing the sequence, the partners must adopt correct range. This is achieved by both taking up their respective starting stances and the attacker closing by sliding gradually forwards, first on one foot, then the other. Whatever technique is to be used, the range must be correct. Partners who stand too far apart will over-reach with their techniques and compensate by lengthening stances. Conversely, if they stand too close, the defender will not have sufficient space in which to respond correctly to the attack and will have to exaggerate his evasion accordingly.

During evasion, the defender must step only so far as is necessary to make the attack miss. Techniques are accurately targeted and, if the attacker aims a straight punch at the face, he is unlikely to miss and hit the stomach! By correct assessment of the attacking technique used, the evasion can remove the target just far enough away to miss. A minimal but effective evasion has the distinct advantage of allowing the defender to remain close enough to the attacker to counter both

quickly and effectively with his defence technique. Time
spent in making good bad distancing is wasted time.

Timing is also very important to the defender. The
attacker holds the initiative and can close distance
quickly before the defender's reaction time allows him
to begin his defence. Therefore, it is of great importance
in all forms of sparring, that the defender receives the
earliest warning of attack. This can come by watching
the attacker's eyes. To launch a strong attack, the
attacker needs to gather his resolve and, in the instant
before he begins the attack, his eyes will suddenly
narrow. As soon as this is detected, an attack can be
expected.

This narrowing of the eyes only occurs when there is
a commitment to attack; it may not show at all with
an uncommitted attack or feint. To learn to detect this
tell-tale sign takes a great deal of practice and pre-
arranged sparring is the ideal method by which to learn
it. The gift of good timing is a valuable one and allows
someone with slow reaction times or poor coordination
to compensate for these deficiencies. After much practice, the defender will be able to sense when the attack
is about to be launched and begin his response
accordingly.

Three-step Sparring

There are several forms of pre-arranged sparring,
though the most common are one- and three-step sparring. In three-step sparring, the attacker makes three
consecutive and identical attacks. He may, for example,
use three front kicks to mid-section, each separated by
the shortest of pauses. The defender will step back each
time, maintaining the correct distance between him and
the attacker while performing a guarding or blocking
movement. On the third attack, he will demonstrate the
agreed defence technique.

Three-step sparring is very useful for developing effective basic techniques. Each sequence allows for three
practice repetitions in practical circumstances. One
which pits face blocks against head punches will provide
excellent experience under realistic conditions for the
improvement of that defence. To practice three-step
sparring in the class, the students divide into two facing
lines. On the instructor's command, one line assumes
the role of attacker and the other side practises the
defence. Having completed one sequence, the roles are
then reversed. To broaden experience, it is a good idea
to exchange partners throughout the practice and this
is done by the student at the end of one line running
down to the other end of his line and everyone on that
side moving one place up. Practice concludes when the
original pair face each other again.

The following are typical three-step sparring sequences:

Face your attacker in ready stance. He steps forwards with his left foot into forward stance and you remain waiting. He then steps forwards and punches to your face. As he does so, step back with your left foot into right forward stance and simultaneously head block with your right arm. After the briefest of pauses, the attacker again steps forwards and punches a second time to your face. Step back with your right foot and head block with your left arm. For the final punch, the attacker once more advances and punches to your face with his right fist. Step back and block this as before but conclude with a reverse punch to the centre of his chest. Withdraw your blocking arm to the hip when making the punch. When the sequence is concluded, withdraw to ready position and change roles.

For the second technique, practise a knife block defence to mid-section punch. Start as above, from attention stance. This time, as your attacker moves forward to punch, step back with your right foot into back stance. Block with augmented left knife block. As he attacks again, step back and block with your right hand. On the third attack, knife block with your left hand once again, then lean over your back leg, swivel your hips while lifting your front foot and drive it out as a side thrusting kick to the centre of his chest.

In the third sequence, the attacker uses a side thrusting kick to mid-section. Step back with your right foot into forward stance and block the kick with mid-section inner block, striking the foot on the Achilles tendon. Block the second kick with right inner block and the third kick with your left hand. On this third move, allow his leg to drop to the inside of your leading leg and reverse punch him to the side of his head.

For the final sequence, the attacker uses a front kick to which you reply with a left foot forwards x-block. Make sure that you do not lean forwards too much during the block and stop the kick well out from the body. Repeat the x-block to the subsequent kicks and, on the final one, complete the sequence with a right back fist into the attacker's face.

One-step Sparring

One-step sparring uses a single attack to which a response is immediately made. The response may consist merely of one technique or several, during the execution of which the attacker remains motionless, frozen in his failed attack. The following sequences are just a few of those which can be made up to train in particular techniques:

In the first, the attacker moves from ready stance into

Figure 131 The attacker moves from ready stance into forward stance

Figure 132 As the attacker steps forward to punch to mid-section, step back on the left foot into right back stance and use inner block

left forward stance (figure 131). As he steps forward to punch to mid-section, step back on your left foot into right back stance and stop the blow using inner block (figure 132). As soon as contact is made with his punch, lash out with your blocking arm and strike him in the side of the face with back fist (figure 133). Then withdraw the fist and bring it across your chest. At the same time, transfer weight forward, so your stance changes from a back stance to straddle. As this transference concludes, drive your right elbow into his ribs, beneath the armpit (figure 134).

In the second sequence, step back with your right foot into back stance and stop his mid-section punch with inner block (figure 135). Withdraw your leading left leg and step forward into straddle stance with the right, so your body comes to lie parallel with the attacker's. Strike down with right knife hand into his groin (figure 136), then retrieve the strike and bend your right elbow before turning your hips into the opponent. Use the turning motion to deliver an elbow strike to his face (figure 137).

The third sequence uses quite a complicated defence in response to a single mid-section lunge punch by the attacker. As he advances forwards on his right leg, step back with your left into a tiger stance. Pick up your right foot and drive it out as a side thrusting kick into his chest (figure 138). Withdraw the foot and continue the natural rotation of your body away from him. Set

Figure 133 Strike the face with back fist

Figure 134 Drive the elbow into the ribs

Figure 135 Inner block from back stance

Figure 136 Stepping through, attack his groin with knife hand

your foot alongside the other (figure 139), then back kick with your left leg to his mid-section (figure 140) before continuing the turn which brings you around and forward facing again. In the fourth technique, the attacker's mid-section front punch is replied to by a right foot crescent kick that sweeps it to the side and produces an opening for a follow-up technique (figure 141, overleaf). The kick is recovered and drops to the floor in front of the supporting leg. The defender transfers weight forwards onto it, twists his hips right around (figure 142, overleaf) and back kicks with his left foot to the attacker's throat (figure 143, overleaf).

Figure 137 Twist, deliver elbow strike

Figure 138 Attack with side kick to mid-section

Figure 139 Set your foot alongside the other and rotate your hips fully away

Figure 140 Conclude with back kick to his mid-section

One-step sparring techniques need not just be used for practising defence techniques; they can also be used to perfect attacks. In the following sequence, the attacker wishes to improve his scissors step/turning kick and snap punch combination. For this type of practice, both partners assume a fighting stance with natural guard (**figure 144,** overleaf). Having set the distance, the attacker scissor steps (**figure 145,** overleaf) and snaps out a rear foot turning kick to the opponent's mid-section (**figure 146,** overleaf). He retrieves the spent kick, dropping it forward into walking stance, using the weight of the falling leg to drive out a left snap punch to the opponent's mid-section (**figure 147,** overleaf).

Figure 141 In the fourth technique, the attacker's mid-section front punch is deflected by crescent kick

Figure 142 The defender transfers his weight forwards onto the supporting leg, twists his hips round . . .

Figure 143 . . . and back kicks to the attacker's throat

Figure 144 Both partners assume fighting stance

Figure 145 The attacker scissor-steps . . .

Figure 146 . . . and snaps out a rear foot turning kick to the opponent's mid-section

Figure 147 The weight of the falling leg is used to drive out a left snap punch to the opponent's mid section

Figure 148 The two fighters begin from opposite stances

Figure 149 A jab off the front hand is made

The second sequence uses two quick body punches to divert the opponent. Note that the two fighters are in opposite stance with the attacker's right foot forwards (**figure 148**). In this position, the defender's body is open to attacks from the left leg. The first attack is a jab off the front hand, with the face well guarded (**figure 149**). The jab is pulled back and a reverse punch quickly follows. The action of the reverse punch pulls the hips forwards and takes weight off the rear foot, the heel of which correspondingly rises (**figure 150**). This same foot is then used for a turning kick to the head (**figure 151**).

Figure 150 Ensuing reverse punch pulls the hips forward and takes weight off the rear foot

Figure 151 This foot then lifts into a turning kick to the head

The whole sequence is very fast and effective, relying on a short series of hip-twists to provide the power for each strike. The two attacks to the body concentrate the defender's attention there and the naturally following turning kick is very likely to find an undefended target.

Self-defence techniques must logically be inserted into this part of the syllabus. They rely upon a set response to a specific attack and so should be practised in exactly the same way as any other form of pre-arranged sparring. However, care must be taken in adapting these to real-life situations since the attacker is never going to freeze once he has delivered his attack.

CHAPTER 11: FREE SPARRING IN TAEKWONDO

Free sparring is unprogrammed fighting between two partners. It is intended to simulate a real combat situation but with certain reservations. The opponent's attack is not known beforehand, so any response to it will reflect the partner's inherent ability at defence and counter-attack. Any exchange of powerful techniques is fraught with danger, so the fighters must be experienced and the techniques they use should be as safe as any can be under those circumstances. Body armour may be worn but this cannot be relied upon to stop all techniques harmlessly. There is no substitute for ability and those with only a very small knowledge of taekwondo should not be allowed to discover their deficiencies the hard way.

A finger thrust to the eyes is a very effective fighting technique, as is a kick to the groin or kneecap. These cannot, however, be adequately controlled for the safety of the fighters and are therefore not allowed. The face is particularly susceptible to injury and so strikes in its general direction, even if they do not contact, are not allowed during free sparring. Although free sparring plays an important part in the practice of taekwondo, it plays *only* a part and is not the be-all and end-all.

Success in Free Sparring

In order to free spar properly, the taekwondo student must be fit. He must have sufficient stamina to last the match through, while maintaining a constant level of effective offence and defence. He must also be capable of maintaining his concentration, so that any slip of his opponent can be turned to immediate advantage before it is recovered. Free sparring is far more than just firing off techniques in wild abandon. It is a carefully executed series of movements, each of which has a purpose.

To succeed in free sparring, the student needs to have motivation – the will to win. If he has this, he will be able to face the strenuous training needed to make him into a success. Without motivation he will not succeed, even though he may well be talented. Talented performers find that everything comes very easy and sooner or later they lose momentum. Those who have to work hard for every grade stand a better chance of

You must master basic techniques before you can safely spar

Timing is an important ingredient in successful sparring

making it to the top since they have both the motivation and the resilience to bounce back from any set-back.

Competitiveness is another factor leading to success. The competitive fighter is not afraid of his opponent and has not lost the match before it begins. He sees himself taking the victory and is not content merely to be a good loser. His self-confidence must not cause him to underestimate his opponent. If he receives a set-back early on in the match, competitiveness will allow him to make an effective come-back. He will attack strongly with as much force as is legally permitted. At no time must he allow his exuberance to spill over so it becomes excessive.

This much comes from within the fighter but more can be added through the good offices of an effective coach. The coach is better able to see his fighter's weak points and suggest remedial action. He will not just turn out a carbon copy of himself, complete with his own strengths and weaknesses, but will discover his fighter's capabilities and develop them. He is able to motivate the athlete to do better and can help him to overcome the sort of depression that can result from a poor performance.

The fighter must respect his coach and look up to him. No holding back or reserve can be permitted if he is to benefit from the coaching given. The coach himself must be able to deal with small numbers of athletes on close terms. Some coaches are better dealing with large classes of novices while others work best with smaller classes of experienced athletes. The free sparring coach is in the latter category.

Training and Improvement

One of the most important things a coach will be able to do is organize a training programme aimed at success in a particular competition or grading. This programme will aim to bring all the necessary elements of fitness and performance together, assembling them so the athlete reaches a peak on the day required. It is impossible to hold a peak of excellence and so timing is critical.

In pursuit of excellence the fighter cannot expect to come home from a full day at work, eat dinner and then go out for training. The body reaches its peak of activity in the early afternoon and that is when training should take place if maximum progress is to be made. Female athletes will find their abilities fluctuating in accordance with their menstrual cycle and may find severe performance 'lows' during its course. They must be prepared for this and ensure they are taking adequate nutritional supplements to maintain them in top physical shape. Additional vitamins appear to have little value as supplements though it is claimed that they can help in the rapid healing of tissues damaged by sparring.

The training facilities must be suitable if progress is to be maintained. Firstly, they must be situated near the athlete's home, so he can train regularly and often. Secondly, they must have the necessary ancillary aides such as a weight-training room or multi-gym. Above all they must be maintained at an adequate temperature to keep the body and limbs warm. Cold training halls do not allow the whole body to warm up properly and can inhibit flexibility training.

The physical preparation for free sparring begins with solitary training. One of the best ways of developing fast consecutive movement (i.e., one technique quicky following another without pause) is to use a full-length mirror. By looking into this and practising techniques, the fighter sees himself through his opponent's eyes and can spot any openings as they occur. Correct usage of the mirror and shadow fighting leads to an improved guard and better anticipation of counter-attacks. When practising techniques against the air, perform them slowly for a time, since this will reveal any errors in form or balance. Fast techniques do not reveal basic faults which must be remedied before a technique can be used successfully in free sparring.

Virtually all taekwondo techniques can be used during free sparring, with the exception of those too dangerous for inclusion. Those which are used must be capable of making hard impacts without injury and so training on the bag is necessary. Because a student can perform a technique adequately against no resistance does not mean he can land it forcefully on a target. Therefore, he must test all his body weapons to ensure they can be used without risk of injury to himself.

Training with a partner is beneficial since there is a limit to what can be achieved by solitary practice. The partner should be a trusted friend and training take place away from onlookers. Because training in this way is relaxed and instructive, each partner will want to try different techniques and there will be a fair amount of discussion as these are first set up, then evaluated for effect. Armour need not be worn since the techniques are delivered without great force.

The fighter must be versatile if he is to cope with the wide variety of sizes and abilities encountered and so he should practise many taekwondo techniques and not just one or two favourite ones. Vigilant opponents will take note of those which appear most frequently and prepare counters to them. Versatility is the ability to fight on your opponent's own ground rather than sticking rigidly to your own fixed system.

Attacking fighters are often weak on defence, so they must develop their ability to block/evade and counter-attack. An attacking fighter who is able to build up his defences until they are the equal of his attacks has in effect doubled his abilities. The converse is also true, of course, and defensive fighters must build up their attacks for the same reason.

Stance

The starting point for the fighter must be his stance. This must be both unspecialized and highly mobile. It must have the maximum number of possibilities for technique usage without time-consuming changes of alignment and weight distribution. It must be capable of rapid movement in all directions since taekwondo is a fast-moving martial art. For these reasons, therefore, a 50 percent weight distribution on either foot is to be favoured.

The fighter should not stand fully facing his opponent

since this provides the latter with a large and inviting target. A completely side-facing stance minimizes the target seen but also reduces the number of techniques which can be used from it without realignment. Somewhere between the two is a sensible compromise, with the body turned 45 degrees to the front.

Positioning

The hands should be kept moving, so they can distract the opponent. The forward guard should be held well away from the body since in this position it is better able to block attacks close to their origin. The rear hand is held back and close to the body. From there it can launch powerful punches. To facilitate this potential, it should not be pulled too far back, otherwise its deployment will be slow and obvious.

Body positioning is also important since, by careful orientation, the opponent's techniques can be made more difficult to use, leaving your own at an advantage. If you stand directly in front of an opponent, both of you will have the same chances to score if you stand off-set to one side or the other, his techniques will be badly angled and cause him to waste time re-aligning them.

Distance is another factor to take into account when fighting to win. The fighter with longer legs is favoured by a longer fighting distance. It is necessary to cut this down by moving in close.

Fighting

As soon as the referee starts the fight, you must begin by assessing your opponent. A few attack feints will produce a reaction from him and, if this is carefully analysed, it will tell you what kind of a fighter he is. If, as you attack, he flinches and appears to move backwards, you can assume he is a nervous fighter and may be easily dominated by hard hitting and relentless attacks. If he comes forward to attack you, then clearly he is an attacking fighter and you should attack him and maintain pressure throughout. If he stands his ground, then he may be a defensive fighter who will need to be drawn into the attack to reveal his weaknesses.

Fighters who lead with their right hand generally have very strong techniques on the left side. When such a fighter faces the more normal left-foot-forward opponent, both are very much open to turning kicks delivered with the rear leg. You should ideally change your stance to match his, if that is possible, and, if it is not, constantly watch your body positioning so you don't move into the centre line of his body where his attacks will be most powerful. Try and ensure you always move to the closed side of his body (on the same side as his leading fist).

Techniques must be
controlled to avoid injury

Fighting techniques

Techniques must always be used in such a way as to enhance their possibility of scoring. The front kick is useful both as an attack in its own right and as a means of pushing the attacker out to a distance where he can be hit with a follow-up technique. Like all taekwondo free sparring techniques, it should be delivered on the move, with perhaps a scissors step beforehand. The kick should strike high on the body and preferably on the same side as the forward guard. The combined effect of this is to make it more difficult to block. The scissors step can be omitted if desired and replaced with a slide forward or slight hop on the supporting leg sufficient to close distance. Use a front foot kick to stop a sudden advance, thereby securing an instant in which to retake the initiative.

A turning kick off the back leg has a long way to travel and so it is correspondingly vulnerable. To reduce the risk of counter-attack, bring your knee up and quickly around to the front of your body where it can ward off any sudden advances. Avoid a great circular motion that tells the opponent in plenty of time what your intentions are. Keep a valid guard and lean your body away from the direction of the kick so an easy target is not presented. The rising knee can also be used to push the opponent back prior to kicking him.

A double turning kick is effective in exploiting an opening. Aim first for the mid-section, taking care to lean away and bring your knee rapidly around. As the kick is pulled back, lash out with it again, this time at the head. During the second kick, the supporting leg turns a few more degrees and allows further hip involvement, resulting in a kick no less powerful than the first. The delivery of two kicks to different and widely separated targets is a sound tactic. The first draws the hands low and the second, following on quickly, finds the unguarded head.

The reverse sequence is not so easy because the high turning kick needs a great deal of hip-twist on the supporting leg to bring it forcefully to its target. None is left to power the second kick which in consequence is too weak to stand a chance of scoring.

An alternative way of creating an opening is by confusing the opponent over what kick is being used. A direct travelling front kick, for example, needs a different counter-response to, say, a turning kick. The opponent's success in avoiding a score on him depends upon seeing, identifying and correctly responding to an attack. If that attack suddenly changes in character, his defence is caught off guard. As an example of this, try a front kick to your opponent's mid-section and, just as the foot is nearing its target, suddenly twist your hips and lift the kicking knee higher. The foot will flip up and around into the side of the opponent's face while he is left looking for a front kick that did not materialize. The converse can also be practised but it is less effective.

Side kicks are best used from a straddle stance with the body turned sideways on. It is possible to kick off the rear leg in a walking or forward stance but the kick takes too long by comparison with the front-leg equivalent. From straddle stance lift your front foot and lean back correspondingly. Drive the kicking leg and, as you do, slide forwards behind the kick on your supporting leg. Twist your hips fully so the supporting foot turns completely away from the direction you are moving and allow that leg to slide forwards. Body movement is important because it adds momentum to the force of the kick. Side kick can be used from quite short distances when the front leg comes within the opponent's forward guard. This makes it extremely difficult to block.

A reverse turning kick is an effective competition technique which, like the turning kick, suffers from an excessively long lead-in during which it is susceptible to counter. Unless you have opened with a diversion, it is a better idea to use hook kick in its place, perhaps with a scissors step or a simple step-up disguised with a front hand jab. Reverse turning kick used on its own is a better counter-attack technique, especially during a fast exchange of techniques.

CHAPTER 12: COMPETITION TAEKWONDO

Taekwondo competition is an athletic activity which makes the severest demands upon the athlete's fitness and competence. The bout may consist of up to three punishing rounds during which time the athlete must maintain the highest standards of fighting ability. Concentration should not lapse for an instant if the maximum usage is to be made of opportunities and openings. Physical resilience is essential in a combat sport where full power attacks are allowed to the face and body. In recognition of these facts, no one below the rank of black belt first dan is allowed to compete at official competitions and no one but officially trained and qualified refereeing personnel may adjudicate.

The Competition Area
The area for a taekwondo competition is a flat square measuring 12 metres along the sides. The competition surface should either be matted or of sprung wood. This is because the vigour of the competition inevitably results in someone falling heavily and a hard floor may make any injuries sustained worse. Where mats are used they must be securely fixed and incapable of moving underfoot. If gaps open up between them, feet can be trapped with consequent risk of injury.

The competition area may be raised on a platform or stage, as long as the height it is raised to does not exceed 20 centimetres. Within the competition area, another square is marked out with sides of 8 metres. This is the actual area of combat and is known as the 'contest area', to distinguish it from the all-inclusive 'competition area'. It is delineated with brightly coloured tape 75 millimetres in width. Standing points for the two contestants and the referee are indicated by tape circles of 15 centimetres diameter.

The contestants' marks are 1 metre each side of the contest area centre point. The referee's mark is 1½ metres from the centre point, at right angles to the two contestants' positions. From this position, the referee can face the juror's table; on his right stands the blue contestant, on his left the red contestant. At each corner of the contest area sit the judges, in a chair situated 50 centimetres from the corner itself. These are numbered in relation to the jury table. The judge to the jury's immediate left is designated '1' and to their immediate right '4'. Judges '2' and '3' occupy respectively the left and right diagonals.

The jury sit at the control table for that area, positioned above a further 15-centimetre circle at least 3 metres from the edge of the contest area and facing the referee. The fighters and their coaches have benches which are 3 metres away from the edge of the contest area behind their respective fighting positions.

Conditions of Entry to Competition
In order to be allowed to compete in taekwondo competition, the contestants must hold headquarters-issued current dan grade certificates and must be members of the club or nationals of the nation competing. In an international match, the fighters will be required to prove their nationality by means of passports. Other entry restrictions can be applied at the discretion of the organizers and it is a sensible idea to contact them and obtain a copy of the rules of entry before participating.

Clothing
Contestants must wear a clean taekwondo training tunic in a good state of repair. Dirty or damaged uniforms reflect discredit upon the sport and practice of taekwondo and cannot be allowed. Over the jacket, body armour of an approved type is worn. This must be kept securely fastened during the bout. Male contestants must wear an approved groin guard. Women may also wear groin guards if they wish.

Approved forearm and shin guards may be worn beneath the tunic and fitted mouthguards are optional.

The contestants should not wear any metal objects which could cause injury to the opponent. For this reason, watches, rings, necklaces, chains and earrings must all be removed. Metal or hard hair grips or clasps cannot be allowed and long hair should be secured with an elastic band. Finger and toenails must be clean and not of such a length ås to risk lacerations during legitimate techniques. The contestants may not wear spectacles, slippers or training shoes during the bout.

Officials
The taekwondo bout is controlled by a referee qualified by the appropriate training committee. First-class referees are generally those of sixth dan ranking who have refereed more than six times in a scheduled international tournament since they received their second-class certificate. Second-class referees must hold at least a fifth dan certificate and should have officiated at least four times since they gained their third-class certificate. Third-class referees are those who hold what is termed a 'Preliminary Referee Certificate'. Once awarded, an

international refereeing qualification remains valid until the holder's fiftieth birthday.

The referee is assisted by four corner judges whose job it is to record scores and penalties as they occur throughout the bout. The judges are all third-class refereeing officials. Where there is a shortage of officials at a tournament, the bout may still operate using only two judges and one member of the jury.

The jury comprises two persons holding a first-class refereeing qualification. They have the authority to examine and if necessary to recommend alteration of an incorrectly given decision by the referee. This alteration may be made during the bout for relatively simple matters – for example, the wrong fighter is inadvertently given the victory or the points have been incorrectly added – or attended to after the bout has concluded.

To confirm impartiality, refereeing officials should not come from the same country or club as either of the contestants. Furthermore they should not occupy any other positions during the operation of a taekwondo tournament. Refereeing officials must wear their official uniforms during the tournament and they are not allowed to wear spectacles.

Since taekwondo is a contest on equal terms between two contestants, the advantages conferred by drug-induced performances cannot be tolerated. There may well be drug tests at a tournament and anyone found with a positive response will face a disciplinary sanction – but in any case he will be disqualified from the competition without hesitation and any honours gained will be forfeit. Taekwondo is an Olympic-recognized sport and, as such, it adheres closely to the International Olympic Committee's rules on doping. The IOC's schedule of prohibited substances has been adopted by taekwondo.

Competition Weight Categories

Individual competition is by weight divisions and the following categories are currently in use:

For Men

Fin weight	− 50 kilos
Fly weight	+ 50/ − 54 kilos
Bantam weight	+ 54/ − 58 kilos
Feather weight	+ 58/ − 64 kilos
Light weight	+ 64/ − 70 kilos
Welter weight	+ 70/ − 76 kilos
Middle weight	+ 76/ − 83 kilos
Heavy weight	+ 83 kilos

For Women

Fin weight	− 43 kilos
Fly weight	+ 43/ − 47 kilos
Bantam weight	+ 47/ − 51 kilos
Feather weight	+ 51/ − 55 kilos
Light weight	+ 55/ − 60 kilos
Welter weight	+ 60/ − 65 kilos
Middle weight	+ 65/ − 70 kilos
Heavy weight	+ 70 kilos

In any competition using full-contact techniques, a weight advantage can be telling. For this reason all contestants are accurately weighed-in before the start of each competition. Those who do not make the weight are disbarred from entry. The draw for a taekwondo competition is random and a straight elimination is used to decide the winners and third places. To ensure a trouble-free elimination, the entry level will be made up to the nearest convenient number. In practice this means randomly inserting what are called 'byes'. Ideally these should not occur next to each other in the draw, but should be evenly spaced throughout the pools (if such are used). For any category of match, at least three entries must be made for it to go ahead. In national competitions it is a good idea if fighters from the same club do not meet each other in the first round and this too may require looking at to avoid contention.

The Bout

In a formal match, each bout will consist of three three-minute rounds, with a one-minute break between each. This may be varied according to the rules of a particular tournament and, if time is short, three two-minute rounds can be fought, with a thirty-second rest between each. During the break, the contestants must leave the contest area and go to their benches. The referee stands quietly in the area and there is no discussion between the members of the refereeing panel.

Time is recorded by a timekeeper who sits at the jury table. He uses a stopwatch and has an audible signal for sounding the end of time. Unless the referee signals for the clock to be stopped for any reason, it will continue until time-up. The round is started by the referee and time begins from that point.

It is always the contestant's responsibility to be at the competition area in time for the bout. Normally three calls will be made for the missing contestant and, after a minute of waiting time, he will be disqualified. Once he arrives, he will take up position on his starting mark and await the direction of the referee. From his start position, the referee calls for formal bows to the jury and between the contestants themselves before announcing the start of the bout. At the end of the bout, the bows are performed in reverse order and an award is made by the referee.

There are several ways to win a taekwondo bout. A win by disqualification is awarded when the opponent has committed a prohibited act of such gravity that he must be disbarred. A win by withdrawal occurs when the opponent is unable or unprepared to fight further. A win through injury occurs when the opponent is unable to continue through injury not caused by prohibited action. A win by knock-out means that the opponent has been stunned or otherwise stopped by a legitimate technique and is not capable of fighting on within the time set by the referee. A win by points occurs at the end of a match when one contestant has amassed more scoring points than his opponent. A win by deduction of points occurs when the contestant has accumulated either six half-point or three one-point penalties and in consequence forfeits the bout. When two contestants are equal in terms of the points they have scored, a verdict can still be made on the grounds of superiority if it is felt that one contestant displayed a better technique or showed a greater attacking spirit.

At the conclusion of a bout in which there has been no disqualification, knock-out etc., the referee collects the judges' score cards and hands them to the jury. After examining the scores, the jury informs the referee of the verdict and he will then announce it.

At any time the referee can stop the bout and award a verdict on his own authority if, for instance, the contestant's coach throws his towel into the contest area, if the tournament doctor says a contestant cannot continue, or if one contestant misbehaves and protests the referee's action. In the latter case, the verdict will be automatically awarded to the opponent, regardless of the standing score at that time, if the referee is unable to re-start the bout after a period of one minute.

Each time the referee breaks the fighting, it is re-started at the same position it was halted. An exception is made when a penalty is imposed. In this instance, the contestants must resume their starting positions.

Scoring

Scores are awarded during the match for clean, skilfully delivered techniques which make contact with the scoring area. The scoring area includes the face and the front and sides of the body. Successful straight punches and kicks can score up to one point but, despite this similarity in score, the kick is more favoured since it is a technically difficult technique. Therefore, in any situation where a bout is tied on points, the contestant who performed the most scoring kicks will be given the decision. A score is also awarded for a skilfully executed legitimate scoring technique which halts and/or stuns the opponent or which knocks him down. Scores can be disallowed if, after earning one, the contestant then falls over, or clinches with his opponent, or tries to prevent him from making a legitimate attack.

Although it is the judges' function to record scores, the referee can signal that a score is invalid when he knows it was made after a command to stop the round or when the fighters were outside the contest area. If the referee believes that a judge has failed to note a penalty, he must raise the matter with the jury and not with the judge concerned. The judges may themselves see an action which they regard as penalizable but they may not draw it to the attention of the referee if he has missed it. Neither should they enter the penalty on their scoresheets without it having been imposed by the referee in his discretion. They can, however, attract the referee's attention if he misses the fact that a fighter has received three one-point or six half-point penalties.

A score will be allowed even if the attacker has his foot on the boundary of the contest area during the delivery though, if it occurs again, the referee should draw the contestant's attention to it. If the contestant scores with a legitimate technique on an opponent who momentarily steps outside the contest area boundary, or who is knocked down outside the boundary, that score will stand.

A knock-down occurs when any part of the contestant other than his feet touch the floor. It is also regarded as knock-down when the contestant staggers and is unable to defend himself. A contestant who is knocked to the floor and then promptly regains his feet is said to have been knocked down. There is no limit to the number of knock-downs that may occur in any taekwondo bout.

A knock-out occurs when a contestant is unable to resume the round after the referee has counted to ten. The referee must take great care to ensure that a knocked-out fighter actually has been knocked out and is not suffering from the effects of, say, a punch in the throat.

Knock-outs or knock-downs must be closely scrutinized since they involve risk of injury to the contestant. If a contestant is hit with a forceful but legitimate technique and either staggers or falls, the referee will immediately stop the round, check the contestant has been genuinely knocked out, send the opponent back to his bench and begin a count. If the injured contestant is unable to resume fighting by the time 'ten' is reached, he will be declared the loser by a knock-out and the doctor summoned. The doctor is always able to advise whether the injured contestant may continue and his advice is always heeded.

If the injured contestant regains his feet by a count of eight, the referee will continue the count to its conclusion and then examine the contestant to confirm that he is fit to continue. If he is, the bout will be allowed to continue. If the contestant rises before the count of eight, the referee continues counting to eight before re-starting the round.

The count will take place regardless of bout time and, even if the end of the round is signalled during the count, it will still continue to its conclusion. If both contestants are knocked to the ground, the referee will begin a count which will continue for as long as one of them remains unable to rise. If both fail to rise, then the verdict will be given to the contestant with the greater number of points at that time.

If a knock-out arises through a foul technique or is delivered after a command to break, the victim will be given the victory and the offender disqualified. If the contestant is kicked in the groin, he is expected to resume fighting within a reasonable time and, if he cannot, he will forfeit the bout. On the other hand, if the referee considers that the disabling groin attack was intentional, he will disqualify the offender. If the referee has any difficulties in deciding the winner, he can raise the matter with the doctor and judges.

Penalties

If a contestant breaks the rules, he can incur a disqualification imposed by the referee (for very serious infractions) or he may be penalized by one point deducted from his final total score. To make this deduction, the referee will halt the bout, return the contestants to their starting points and impose the penalty in the clear view of the judges and jury. If the contestant incurs three separate point deductions, he will forfeit the bout.

To incur this penalty, the fighter must have committed a serious breach of the rules. The following are serious breaches: attacking the fallen opponent, causing injury to the opponent's face through a punch, head butting, intentional attack after the referee has called for a break in fighting, uttering uncalled-for comments, and behaving in a manner likely to reflect discredit upon taekwondo. A point may also be deducted if the competitor leaves the 12-metre competition area.

Half-point penalties may be imposed by the referee in the form of warnings for less serious rule infractions. The accumulated half points are subtracted from that contestant's final total score. After six such warnings, the contestant forfeits the bout.

Half-point penalties can be imposed for holding on to the opponent, turning one's back on the opponent to escape his attack, purposefully falling down, purposefully exiting from the 8-metre contest area, attacking with the knee, throwing the opponent, feigning injury to gain tactical advantage, back-pedalling and refusing to engage in meaningful combat, attacking the groin, punching to the face, pushing the opponent, and generally behaving badly.

The coach must also behave correctly, or he may well incur penalty for his contestant. In particular, he is not allowed to shout directions during the operation of the bout. Supporters or the contestant's team-mates are also constrained to behave themselves and, if they do not, their contestant can lose a full point.

Whenever an injury is caused to one or both of the contestants, the referee will halt the round and stop the time by informing the timekeeper clearly of his intentions. He will then examine the injury caused and will decide whether or not it is feasible to resume the round. If this proves impossible, he will disqualify the contestant who caused the injury and award the verdict to the injured party, unless the injured party has caused the injury to himself. In this case, he shall forfeit the bout and the verdict will be given to his opponent.

If the bout can be re-started, the referee will allow the injured party time to receive first aid treatment and impose a penalty where necessary. If he considers the contestant is fit to resume fighting but the latter expresses no will to do so, then he will forfeit the bout. Contestants may wear bandages as a result of injuries sustained during the tournament but for no other reason. If the doctor advises that a contestant is in actual physical danger because he is physically unable to defend himself adequately against his opponent, then the referee will listen to the suggestion and decide upon it.

All protests concerning decisions made must be put in writing and submitted to the arbitration board appointed for that tournament.

CHAPTER 13: TAEKWONDO DESTRUCTION TECHNIQUES

Taekwondo is unique among all the large schools of international martial art in its attention to breaking techniques. Testing the efficiency of strikes, kicks and punches by applying them to boards, tiles and bricks as a requirement for grading is uniquely Korean. Most people think of destruction techniques as a spectacular manifestation of Japanese karate but nothing could be further from the truth. The only school of karate to lay any emphasis at all on breaking is one founded by a Korean.

In any martial art using blows and kicks as weapons, it is essential that they be effective. A less practically minded fighting art might regard the effectiveness or otherwise of its blows as academic, but taekwondo is a valid military form of unarmed combat, to be used when other weapons are unavailable. Therefore, its own weapons must be as effective within their natural limitations as the bullet and bayonet. The theory of the actions must be measured by their actual performance.

It is easy to punch and kick savagely at the air and not that much more difficult to strike a soft punchbag, but striking full force into something hard is quite another thing. The untrained knuckles are covered only with a thin layer of skin and the wrist may not be in quite the right configuration to transmit impact power without flexing and breaking. Can the soldier be sure that when he strikes someone with full force he is not going to damage his hands badly?

Conditioning the Hands and Feet
The answer lies in the development of a testing programme that clearly shows the effectiveness of taekwondo techniques. The hands and feet have to be turned into effective bludgeons, capable of causing severe injury to an opponent through repeated full-force strikes, without themselves becoming injured in the process.

Testing and conditioning programmes have long been in existence. Their purpose is to make the hands and feet capable of withstanding injury when they are used as weapons. This can be achieved in two ways. One way is to develop thick layers of calloused skin over bony structures and the other is to develop callous on the bones themselves. The former is the less damaging way. To thicken the skin, the existing covering must be shown to be inadequate. Anyone who has worn a pair of loose shoes will know that constant abrasion causes blisters but, when they burst and new skin forms, that new skin is always thicker and more resistant to abrasion.

The feet are relatively easy to condition since their major striking surfaces are already covered in a thick layer of calloused skin. Simply walking about barefoot on a variety of surfaces can build up callous to the extent where the delicate bones are cushioned. The hands are more difficult to condition. They can be conditioned by using a punching post which flexes under impact and whose target pad is comprised of a rough material such as wheat straw. After punching at this pad for a while, the skin becomes red and lacerated. The next day the process can be repeated and so on until the skin on the knuckles begins to coarsen.

Consistent training in this manner will raise large pads of skin callous over the knuckles, yet leave the fingers capable of fine movement. The only problem with skin callous is that it can be torn off and, if conditioning is not consistent, it thins and becomes ineffective. It is for these reasons that most people build up bone callous.

To do this, the same training is used except that the punching post is not so flexible and the impact pad is uncushioned. Pounding at this bruises the knuckles and causes actual injury to the underlying bones. To compensate for this recurring damage, the body lays down new deposits of bone at the sight of the injury, making the knuckles heavier and more prominent. Bone conditioning is more painful but its effects are longer lasting.

Suitable Materials for Breaks

Having produced the weapons, the next thing to do is test them. It is not a good idea to hit another person full force and so substitutes have to be found. These must be hard, yet capable of yielding to a strong impact. The normal substitutes in use are pine boards, bricks, breeze and cement building blocks and roofing tiles. Some people also break blocks of ice, others pieces of stone. Whatever is selected must be rigid, have little tensile strength, not flex unduly on impact and require a fair degree of force before it breaks.

The target of a destruction test breaks because it is deformed beyond its natural flexibility by an impact and cannot recover. A piece of willow is difficult to break because its flexibility is so great as to allow a great deal of deformation before permanent damage occurs. On the other hand, a sheet of glass is extremely hard but shatters easily because its structure does not permit more than a tiny amount of flexion.

It helps if the material has a line along which it is most likely to break. A piece of wood, for example, will always break easiest with the grain. Stone, too, has planes of cleavage along which it will fracture if struck hard enough. The clever part lies in discovering those planes. Other materials have a granular structure in which the particles are not strongly bonded together – such as in a brieze block. The latter is made from compressed ash and, as long as it is well supported along its length, will withstand a great deal of weight. If the support is slightly inadequate, however, it will easily break.

Bricks also have a granular structure and, when new, are brittle and easily broken. Roof tiles are both wide and long in comparison with their thickness and can be shattered with little problem. Chipboard is made from sawdust mixed with a strong glue. The glue becomes hard when dry and will allow the board to break under a sharp impact.

Softer materials are often the most difficult to break. Obechi wood, for example, is only slightly heavier than balsa and as soft to work. Even an unconditioned fist can punch it with full power and not suffer injury. It has a well-developed grain along which one might expect it to fracture easily but, because of its very softness, the wood yields and compresses on sudden impact, dispersing energy before it can build to that needed to cause fracture. Whereas brittle materials can be broken with a sharp, fast rap, softer materials need a heavy and penetrating impact.

Whatever material is chosen, it must be dry. Dampness causes swelling of the fibres of wood and makes them far more resistant to breaking. A piece of 25-millimetre-thick pine board can be easily broken when dry but, once wet, it can defy all attempts. Similarly, a brick straight from the kiln can be shattered fairly easily but one which has faced the elements, lying in a builder's yard for a couple of months, will need a 7-pound sledgehammer.

The Target
The shape of the target is also a factor to consider. Ideally it should be oblong, with the grain (if it is wood) running across the width. An oblong board is easier to break than a square board simply because, if it is supported correctly, the line of fracture is short in relation to the amount of wood. For an easy break, the cleavage plane must always cover the shortest distance

in relation to the size of the material chosen.

Holding and arranging the target

The method of holding the target during the break will depend upon the choice of target material. Very hard and brittle materials can be broken unsupported. A new and dry brick needs only to be held at its base to be broken with a knife hand strike. Dry parana pine can be suspended from a piece of cotton or even dropped through the air and broken. In these cases, the blow must be very fast and strike with the sharpest of raps. Softer or thicker materials require more careful mounting so that they don't move on impact, since this can absorb much of the force applied. Solid ground makes the most efficient support but other, albeit less effective, supports can be used.

When the material is held by people, certain rules should be obeyed. Brittle items may be held by one person but a fair thickness of more resilient material requires at least two. They must both adopt forward stances, with weight pressing down on the front foot. The rear foot is locked straight, as are the elbows. One partner leads with his right foot to the centre, the other with his left foot. The material is held on the palm heels with the fingers just curling around to rest on the very edge for steadying it. Under no circumstances should the supporting fingers actually come to lie over the target since they will surely be hit. Additional helpers may be positioned so they can reach and steady the wood-holding wrists.

The items to be broken must be carefully aligned in the grip and, if square boards of wood are used, they must all be aligned in the same way, so that in one board the grain does not run at right angles to that in the next. Such an arrangement would make destruction impossible to all but the strongest of people. Care must also be taken to ensure that the material will break the correct way and not trap unwary hands or feet. For example, when breaking hand-held boards with a punch, it is best to have the wood grain running vertically since, when this snaps, it curls around the sides of the fist and doesn't lacerate knuckles and fingers. When breaking a slab of ice using a punch, the fist must be left among the shards for a second or two. By this means, the hand's warmth will melt any razor edges lurking close by.

The angle of the material must be carefully arranged to ensure a direct impact. Striking an angled board can cause a fist to ricochet off, shedding callous and underlying tissue on the way. It is human nature for the target-holders to flinch and, in so doing, they can inadvertently alter the angle of attack and in some cases move the target by 5 or 6 centimetres. The effect of this on a carefully targeted blow can be substantial.

In any hand-held break, it is necessary to work out which way the pieces will fly. In a crowded demonstration, the person who kicks and shatters roofing tiles with an overhead kick may find sharp pieces flying far and wide into the upturned faces of his audience. All breaking should be done on a tarpaulin of sufficient size since broken shards and splinters can imbed themselves in expensive mats and polished floors, wreaking havoc on the surface and feet alike. It is always a good idea to take a broom and plastic bin to collect the debris after any breaking demonstration.

To allow maximum deformation of an oblong target, it must be held at either end of its length, rather than its width. Therefore, a piece of wood measuring 25 centimetres by 10 centimetres by 25 millimetres, with the grain running across the width, will break easily across that width but not across its length. A square target can be held either way, within the constraints given above. Therefore, before attempting any kind of break, examine the material and ensure it is correctly supported to break in a convenient and safe manner.

Maximum Effect and Minimum Force
An easier way to break enormous thicknesses of brittle material, for example, a stack of brieze blocks, is to use spacers. Put two bricks on the solid ground (not on a stage or resilient surface) and lay the first brieze block so that only the very extremities of its length rest on the supports. Then take a piece of 1-centimetre dowelling and place this on the upper surface of the block, directly above the brick supports. Lay the next brieze block over this and so on until the required number have been added. Now, when the first block is broken, its ends drive down into the second block, fracturing it and so on until the whole pile lies shattered. The energy needed to achieve this spectacular break is scarcely more than that required to break just one block. It must be said, however, that there are people who are quite capable of breaking great thicknesses of material without the use of dowels.

Destruction Techniques
Ideally, the capability of each powerful technique in taekwondo's armoury should be tested by means of a destruction test. The materials selected for the test must be such as realistically to assess that technique. Therefore, the test for a hammer fist will be considerably more rigorous than that for spear hand. The hammer fist is perhaps the ideal technique to gain an introduction to taekwondo destruction training. Start by using

a brieze block supported off the floor by bricks. A cloth can be draped over the block, to avoid the possibility of sharp pieces penetrating the wrist.

Drop on your right knee (assuming you wish to break the block with your right hand) and extend your left hand. Rehearse the breaking action a couple of times, lowering your clenched fist to the block, then raising it up and back before bringing it down again. As it descends, lean forwards slightly into the blow and strongly pull back your left hand to the hip, closing it into a tight fist as you do so. When you are confident, take a deep breath and smash down at the block with all your force. Aim to smash right through it and tense your whole body on impact.

To break with the fist, start with 1 inch of dry, oblong pine board held firmly by two trusted assistants. When you are satisfied that it is correctly positioned and angled, take up a left forward or walking stance (assuming you will wish to break the board with your right fist) that is close enough for you to reach the target without having to lean forward. Your punching arm should be nearly, but not quite, straight on contact. Rehearse the move until you feel confident to try for the break.

Withdraw your right side and extend your left arm forward, so it is almost touching the board, then twist your hips into the target, driving out your fist as strongly as possible. Pull back the left hand at the same time and close both into tight fists before impact. Shift your body weight forwards behind the punch and do not halt on first contact with the wood. Provided you have harnessed the power effectively, you will smash straight through the board. It is not a good idea to twist your fist actually on impact, since this can tear the knuckles.

For knife hand, try a dry, new brick held firmly. Stand in a straddle stance with your right shoulder to the left of the brick. Put your right knife hand palm down against the brick, then withdraw it by bending the elbow and bringing the palm to your left ear. Twist your upper body to the left and then let it pull around straight again, using the twist to drive the knife hand around and into the target. The hand turns palm down in the instant before contact is made with the brick.

Rehearsing

Rehearse the move several times, using your left arm to augment the movement. Extend it far out and behind the body before gathering it close in support of the right hand. When you are ready, wind the body back and release the strike, aiming to cut right through the brick without so much as a falter. Ensure you contact the brick with the correct part of knife hand, otherwise the bones of the wrist can be chipped.

Front kick can be tested for the first time against a hand-held, brittle board. For a single board, only one assistant is necessary since the kick develops a great surplus of power. The board should be held with straight arms to correct angle and arranged so that, when it smashes, it does not close around the top and bottom of the foot. Measure the kick against the board and rehearse the movement slowly until you are confident. Then drive the kick out, using your hips to lift it up and through the board.

Avoid rehearsing too vigorously on a single board or thin piece of brittle material. A premature fracture can ruin your carefully planned demonstration. At the other end of the scale, do not run the risk of bad injury by repeatedly pounding at a piece of material that will not break. Make it a rule never to try more than two impacts with one technique. If you have tried unsuccessfully to break three boards, throw one away after the first strike and try again. If this too fails, then use a different technique. Be prepared to abandon a break if the material is obviously unsuitable.

Do not break with head butt. This technique can cause brain damage and, if repeated too many times, will result in long-standing detrimental effects. The second 'do not' concerns children. Their bones are growing and can be seriously damaged by any form of destruction training. Even press-ups on the knuckles or backs of the wrists can cause damage.

CHAPTER 14: FITNESS FOR TAEKWONDO

To get all the benefits from taekwondo training, it is necessary to be fit enough. Students who find themselves preoccupied with merely lasting through the lesson will miss much of the technique and progress more slowly than their fitter colleagues. Ideally the mind should be free to concentrate on what is being taught. Lasting out the session should present no problem and neither should there be any problem in following the range of movements taught. To achieve these ideals, the taekwondo student needs to be fit.

Fitness simply means being physically and mentally able to perform a set task. The fit taekwondo athlete will find no challenge in keeping up with the training because he has developed an adequate level of fitness. Fitness is no simple thing, though. It exists at different levels and in many forms.

The experienced taekwondo student will have a high level of the correct type of fitness to benefit training. He may not, for instance, be fit enough to lift heavy weights but, since that doesn't form part of training in taekwondo anyway, he won't miss it. He may not be able to run the marathon in a record time and quite probably will not rival a trained sprinter in the 100-metre dash yet, paradoxically, will still be ideally fit for taekwondo. This is because each activity demands a certain mix of the characteristics which together constitute the beneficial condition of being fit. The clever part comes in deciding the correct mix for taekwondo.

Aerobic Fitness
The first element needed is undoubtedly a reasonable level of what is called 'aerobic fitness'. In fact, aerobic fitness provides a platform upon which the other requirements of fitness must be assembled. It is the ability of the body to perform a reasonable level of fairly undemanding work over an extended period and is so named because of its demands upon the cardio-vascular system.

Sufficient oxygen must be taken in and carbon dioxide removed to keep the muscles working well. In the absence of adequate oxygen, the muscle is able to work without it ('anaerobically') by breaking down its food source to lactic acid, instead of carbon dioxide. This unfortunately builds up in the muscle and leads to a cumulative loss in efficiency. After a while, the muscle becomes stiff, loses the power to contract effectively and exhaustion sets in.

Aerobic fitness involves a build-up in capability of the lungs and heart, so they are able to shift more and better oxygenated blood. By this means, the accumulation of lactic acid is slowed and the onset of fatigue correspondingly delayed.

To achieve an adequate level of this kind of fitness, the taekwondo athlete must run or swim a minimum of three twenty-minute sessions a week. The object of this is to raise the heart rate to the safe maximum that can be sustained by the student; this figure will vary according to age. To calculate the safe maximum, subtract twenty from the person's age and subtract the result from 170. Thus, for a forty-year-old in training, the safe maximum sustainable heart rate would be 150 beats per minute. A programme that produces this rate will rapidly improve that particular athlete's aerobic capability.

Anaerobic Fitness
Certain types of exercise are extremely local in the muscles they involve and do not impose demands upon the cardio-vascular system. Weight training, for example, is designed to develop discrete muscle groups and, though constant repetition of one exercise will cause exhaustion in the muscle concerned, the rest of the body remains relatively unconcerned. In this instance, loading on the muscle exceeds its capabilities and exhaustion sets in. A specific exercise to develop that muscle's endurance will make it more capable of tolerating the inevitable build-up in lactic acid so it can operate for longer and harder than the untrained equivalent. This kind of fitness is referred to as 'anaerobic' and it is another necessary inclusion within the taekwondo athlete's overall fitness programme.

The practice of taekwondo requires sustained and powerful punching and kicking. The person who can maintain a strenuous and forceful attack over a long period is making a strong contribution to his chances of success in competition. Therefore, the taekwondo athlete must train and develop the muscles used in punching and kicking.

Constant repetition of related movements under loaded conditions will increase force and train the body in the execution of correct techniques. Anaerobic fitness of the type required is best generated through circuit training comprising relevant exercises. The athlete must complete a set of one exercise before moving to the next set, always competing against the clock. The object is to get around three circuits as quickly as possible and, once this can be done in reasonable time, the number of exercises in each set can be increased.

The type of exercise will reflect the taekwondo athlete's needs. He may, for example, attach a strong piece of elastic to wall bars and do twenty punches while holding it in tension. He might then do twenty weighted squats to develop the muscles used in kicking out with the lower leg. Whatever the exercises chosen, they must follow each other rapidly, giving little opportunity for the fatigued muscle to recover.

The Suppleness Programme

Taekwondo fitness involves more than strength and stamina. It also needs flexibility – especially in the hips. Therefore, a suppleness programme must go hand in hand with development of muscle strength. This programme includes exercises designed specifically to increase the range of movement at a joint by regularly taking that joint through its full range of movement.

Suppleness exercises must not be performed in isolation; they only come into their own in conjunction with a strength-building programme. Strong muscles exert a stabilizing influence on joints and a programme which develops flexibility without attendant strength can result in joint instabilities.

Suppleness is a function of many factors. Body fat can reduce suppleness by adding so much bulk that it is difficult on purely physical grounds to move a joint through its full range. The fat person may find it impossible to touch his chin to his knees during stretch exercises simply because of the very size of his stomach. The joints themselves have a limit of movement imposed by their structure and this limit can be further reduced by the associated muscles, tendons and ligaments.

Flexibility

Voluntary muscles are elongated fleshy sacs. As a result of nervous stimulation, they contract and produce movement. Their force is transmitted through inelastic strips of specialized connective tissue called tendons. Ligaments support joints and are comprised of a more elastic type of connective tissue. The state of tension in the muscles and tendons is detected by means of what are called 'proprioceptors'. These are specialized structures found in both. They are well supplied with nerve fibres and appear to be one of the major factors affecting flexibility. The resting muscle has certain fibres always under contraction and this produces what is known as muscle tone or 'tonus'.

Most stretching takes place within the belly of the muscle itself. As the muscle is stretched, the proprioceptors send messages back to the central nervous system and attempt to contract the muscle back to its normal resting length. After exercise, the muscles are well supplied with blood and oxygen and are more amenable to stretching. The body should therefore be thoroughly warmed up before any flexibility work is commenced. Stretching a muscle that is not properly prepared will achieve less and may actually incur injury.

The joint must be stretched in the correct way, so that all the pull is on the muscle and not on the joint or tendons. Pressure must be gradually applied up to the previous limit of stretch and held there for at least ten seconds. Provided the pressure is applied gradually to a warm and relaxed muscle, the proprioceptors will accommodate to the stretch and not fight against it. On the other hand, sharp increases in stretch will antagonize the proprioceptors, cause muscle contraction and inhibit further stretching. If the fully stretched muscle is contracted as far as is possible without changing position and then relaxed, a further few degrees of movement will be obtained. The contraction of the stretched muscle seems to fool the proprioceptors into permitting a little more extension.

While it is a good idea to do some flexibility work before the session, the main part of the programme will begin during the cool-down period at the end, when the body tissues are being returned to a more quiescent state. At this time, they will be fully warm and used to the ballistic stretching caused by kicking during training. The suppleness programme should not be confined only to the club. If the student wants to see a good and rapid improvement, he must work at it every day.

Speed

Speed is another important fitness factor for taekwondo. A technique must be fast enough to beat the block or evasion if it is to score. Speed in this context refers not only to limb speed, but to whole body speed too. Reaction time plays an important role in the speed of techniques. It is that period between the first perception of a stimulus such as an approaching punch and the response to it – i.e., a block. To a degree this appears to be inbuilt though exercises which teach hand-to-eye coordination and speed/skill combinations can improve it. The concentration required, though, is high and rapid mental fatigue soon causes a drop-off in efficiency. The use of target mitts is a good way of improving reaction time towards its maximum realization. Speed is not something that can be maintained and training should be so arranged as to allow the taekwondo athlete to reach his maximum speed in time for a selected competition.

Limb speed can be increased by loading the movement concerned. Sprinters train for increased speed by running through sand or water. Resistance to the actions causes a short-lived increase in speed when that resistance is removed. Therefore, to increase speed in punching, for example, the taekwondo athlete can resort to the muscle-developing exercise of attaching a strong elastic to the wall bars and repeatedly punching as quickly as possible.

An Exercise Programme

The following programme of simple exercises will build strength and suppleness for taekwondo training. They should be worked at for at least twenty minutes per day for a minimum of three days a week if a good improvement is desired. They are additional to the road-work or swimming necessary to build aerobic fitness.

Running on the spot

The first exercise consists of running on the spot and raising the knees and elbows as high as possible. The pace should gradually accelerate to a full sprint and be held until breathless. If two of you are training together, face each other and introduce an element of competition into it. After a brief pause to recover your breath, drop into press-up position.

Press-ups

Hold your upper body off the floor on straight arms and rest on the balls of your feet (**figure 152**). Keep the back straight and bend your elbows so that your chest comes to brush the ground. It is important to look forwards, not at the ground, and the backside should not be shoved up into the air (**figure 153**, overleaf).

Figure 152 Keep your back straight and lock your elbows when beginning press-ups

Without pausing at the lowest position, straighten your arms and push the body back up to the start position. Perform this at least twenty times, always keeping your back perfectly straight.

Figure 153 Lower your body until your chest brushes the ground

It is a fact that many women cannot do press-ups. This is due simply to poor chest muscle development in comparison to men. Nevertheless, a woman can still practise press-ups if she drops her knees to the ground.

For those who can manage press-ups easily, try putting one hand over the other in the forward centre line and then bending both elbows. This heavily loads the triceps muscle and many people are unable to push their way back up off the floor. A further variant is the one-armed press-up. To do this properly, the legs must be spread widely to give balance. The upper body twists to the side and the lower arm reaches down to the floor. The other arm rests along the thigh. The object is fully to bend and straighten the supporting arm at least ten times before changing to the other side.

Press-ups can be performed on the knuckles, on the fingertips, on the palms and on the backs of the wrists. Regular press-ups on the knuckles will force back the fingers and help form an effective fist. Children should not be made to do press-ups on the knuckles.

Sits-ups

After press-ups, sit down and lie back, with your hands behind your head. Draw up your feet and, keeping the knees bent, sit up off the floor (**figure 154**), raising your shoulders up and touching your knees with the forehead. If your upper body is heavy, it will be difficult to keep the feet on the floor and they can be anchored beneath a wall bar or something similar. If you are exercising with a partner, link your legs so that one lays over and the other under your partner's.

Figure 154 Always bend your knees when doing sit-ups

Figure 155 Twist your shoulders as you sit up

When you become good at this exercise, introduce a little variation by twisting your trunk as you come up and touching each knee with the opposite elbow (**figure 155**).

Back arches

Roll over onto your stomach and clasp your hands behind your back. Arch your body as high as possible, lifting both feet and chest from the floor. Hold this position for a count of three and then relax back.

Burpees

Next, assume a crouching position, with the palms of your hands resting (**figure 156**). Then shoot your legs out behind you (**figure 157**) and, without pausing, bring them back up and resume the crouch position (**figure 158**). Straighten your legs and, as you rise, front kick high with each leg before sinking down to resume the cycle (**figures 159, 160**). This exercise is called the burpee.

Figure 156 Begin the burpee from a crouch

Figure 157 Shoot your legs out backwards . . .

Figure 158 . . . then pull back into a crouch

Figure 159 Straighten your legs and do a front kick first on one leg . . .

Figure 160 . . . then on the other

Fireman's lift

Fireman's lift is a good leg-strengthener as long as the knees are not taken past 90 degrees. Take someone's right wrist in your left hand and put your right arm between their legs. Drape them over your shoulder and grasp their right wrist with your right hand. With this weight across your back, bend your knees to a right angle and then drop back down again. It is a good idea to do the exercise from a sitting position in a chair. This prevents the knees from bending too far, whereupon the exercise becomes damaging.

Stretching exercises

By this time, the body is well warmed up and ready for the supling programme. Begin by sitting with your legs straight out in front of you and your knees together (figure 161). Let your upper body reach forward and down, keeping your eyes fixed on your feet. Make sure you bend from the lower back and do not merely hunch your shoulders (figure 162). Alternatively, stretch your hands forward as far as you can and try to extend the fingertips well beyond your toes. Remember to keep your head up and bend from the lower back. Do not let your knees rise from the floor. When you have reached your lowest position, hold it and tense the muscles in your leg for a count of ten, then relax them and try for a further increment of stretch. Hold your lowest position for a second count of ten.

Figure 161 Keep the backs of the legs flat on the floor

Figure 162 Keep your knees straight and bend from the lower back

An alternative to this exercise involves taking hold of the balls of your feet and pulling the heels clear of the floor. This can be modified further by starting with the foot gathered in and then extending it to its full length while maintaining your grip on the sole. Holding the foot with the opposite hand increases stretch. It is also possible to crouch down and put your hands under your heels. Then stand up and straighten the knees, hold for a count of ten and sink back down.

Open leg stretches are very important in developing the kind of hip flexibility needed to perform the high kicks so frequently encountered in taekwondo. Sit down as before, but this time spread your legs as widely as possible. Drop your body well forwards and reach out as far as you can. Keep your body low and swing it first to one side, then to the other, touching the ankles on each sweep. Alternatively, grasp your ankles and lean forward (**figure 163**), then return your body to

Figure 163 Don't allow your knees to bend

the upright position, dropping your head to each knee alternately and using the ankle grasp smoothly to pull the body down (**figures 164, 165**). Hold each lowest position for a full count of ten. At no time must the knees rise from the floor.

A particularly effective stretch uses gravity to achieve quite spectacular results. Lie back and arrange it so that your bottom butts up against the wall. Bring your legs together and extend them straight up, pressing lightly against the wall. Then let them open to their maximum and hold them there, while trying to relax the muscles. As they relax, so the legs will spread under the influence

Figure 164 First bend to one side, hold . . .

Figure 165 . . . then bend to the other side

of gravity. They are quite heavy and the pressure exerted on the hip joint can be surprisingly high. The gradual loading, however, minimizes the painful effects of this stretch. Take care to ensure that weight presses down through the hips by remaining as close to the wall as possible. From time to time, tense the muscles of the leg and then relax them. You will be able to see for yourself just how effective this is in squeezing the last inch or two of stretch.

The figure-four leg stretch is particularly good for taking the hip through its full range of movement. Sit upright and extend one leg out in front, pulling the other back and behind to make a right angle. The toes of the extended leg point straight upwards and the retracted leg is pulled fully back against the thigh, making a full 90-degree angle (**figure 166**, overleaf). The first stretch is made in the forwards direction and the chin is lowered until it brushes the knee (**figure 167**, overleaf). Hold this for a count of ten and then bring your body up, around and down into the centre line between the two knees (**figure 168**, overleaf). Reach forward as far as possible and hold this for the count. Return to an upright position and then fold towards the rear knee, attempting to touch it with your forehead (**figure 169**, overleaf). Finally, lie straight back, keeping the body flat on the floor for a count of ten (**figure 170**, overleaf). Repeat on the other leg.

Gather both legs in and sit with them drawn up, soles

Figure 166 Extend one leg and pull the other right back

Figure 167 Lean over the front leg

Figure 168 Then lean between the knees

Figure 169 Then lean over the rear leg

Figure 170 Finally lean straight back

touching. Then try and lower your knees to the floor. Using a partner to apply constant, judicious pressure is extremely beneficial and will produce better results. A partner is very useful in all of these exercises since he can provide the force needed to hold a particular stretch, allowing you singlemindedly to concentrate on relaxation. The force he applies should be smooth, progressive, with no jerks but, above all, he must ease off when told to do so.

Back Exercises
Step forward on your right leg and rest your hands on your hips. Then lean back as far as you can. Change legs and repeat. Next turn your upper body as far to one side as possible, craning your neck to look around and behind you. Hold this position, then swing back and through, turning the other way. Complete the spine exercises by spreading your feet for good balance and leaning forward, so your fingers touch the floor. Swing your body around to the side, describing as wide a circle as possible. At the top of the circle, lean back as far as you can and continue on round until your fingers once more graze the floor. Then swing the other way, repeating the complete exercise several times.

Neck exercises
Finish the work-out with neck exercises. Look to the right, twisting your neck as far as possible, then to the left. Repeat this five times, then lean your head from side to side. Finally, roll your head forward and down, so your chin touches your chest. Take it up in a wide circle, over the shoulder, straight back and around the other side. Once the start position is regained, rotate your head the other way.

When doing these exercises, remember to work within your own limitations and don't overdo it.

CHAPTER 15: SAFETY IN TAEKWONDO TRAINING

Taekwondo is an extremely vigorous activity by any sporting standards. As such, it makes substantial physical demands upon the body. To maintain performance, the lungs must efficiently ventilate the blood and the heart must pump that enriched blood to the working muscles of the body. Furthermore, both must work at a rate that will supply demand. Consequently, students practising taekwondo must be fit enough to do so.

The average person will not have enough capacity to cope with the demands of training and so must be introduced to it gradually if serious physical stress is to be avoided. The heart is a specialized muscle and, like all muscles, if it is not exercised, becomes flabby and inefficient. People who are not used to physical exercise must therefore be careful not to strain themselves by trying to keep up with the more experienced class.

Safety and the Less Physically Fit
Students above the age of forty who want to take up taekwondo will need a more gradual introduction than younger people. With age comes a natural gradual deterioration in function which sensible exercise of the right kind can slow. A sudden plunge into hard training by such persons can load the heart beyond its capabilities and damage may ensue.

This is not to say that older people cannot practise taekwondo; of course they can. It's just that they must be more careful. It is always a good idea for a mature student to have a medical examination before starting. Chances are he won't have had one for years and will be as ignorant about his own state of health as is the instructor he's applied to for membership. By listening to the heart and lungs, the doctor will be able to detect any gross abnormality that training will aggravate.

Students with heart trouble can, however, benefit from taekwondo training. Regular exercise keeps the heart from deteriorating but the watchword here is *don't overdo it*. Provided the instructor is aware of the student's health condition, he can monitor performance and ensure that no excessive demands are imposed.

Uncontrolled taekwondo techniques can be dangerous!

The student himself must be made aware that it is neither clever nor brave to ignore the symptoms of breathlessness or chest pain that can accompany over-exertion. The student who regularly does this will suffer for it sooner or later. On the other hand, the student must be aware of natural breathlessness which comes about in the healthiest of people and is clearly not a sign of impending trouble. Fortunately, most cardiac sufferers are knowledgeable about their illness and will know their limitations. They must always keep medication within easy reach.

The lungs are specially developed to ensure that the maximum volume of air comes in contact with the maximum volume of blood. By this means, carbon dioxide diffuses out and life-giving oxygen diffuses in. The mechanism of breathing in (inspiration) and out (exhalation) is partly controlled by muscular action in the ribs and diaphragm and regular exercise is needed if they are to cope with training demands.

The sedentary person uses only a small amount of lung volume and seldom during the course of the day inflates the lungs to their fullest extent. After many years, such habits can lead to inelastic lungs with consequent reduced volume of air moved in and out. Smoking has a bad effect upon lung tissue and the serious taek-wondo athlete, in consequence, does not smoke.

Illness and taekwondo training

To meet the demands of taekwondo practice, the lungs must work at a high level of efficiency and those diseases which affect them can result in decreased performance. During an attack, asthma sufferers have difficulty breathing out, so consequently they feel breathless. Like the cardiac sufferer, they must be able to distinguish between normal and asthmatic breathlessness and keep medication at hand for when an attack comes on. It appears that the practice of taekwondo can actually improve breathing in asthmatics. The demands made upon the lungs seem to improve their efficiency and actually lead to a reduction in attacks.

Haemophiliacs are people who suffer from uncontrolled bleeding. Their blood is deficient in clotting factors and the slightest of injuries can result in severe bleeding, requiring hospital intervention to save life. Even practice of the techniques themselves can be dangerous. The stretching and kicking can produce slight damage at the joints, resulting in bleeding. It is for this reason that haemophiliacs must never practise taekwondo. 'Partial' haemophilias can also prove dangerous and medical advice is mandatory before training is allowed.

Epilepsy is no bar to training, except where the

sufferer experiences the grand mal type of seizure and the floor of the training hall is unpadded. A grand mal seizure can drop the sufferer violently on the floor and the head is often the first part to make contact. The sufferer sometimes thrashes about and can seriously disrupt the evening's training. After such an attack, the student must be taken home by a friend or another student.

Fortunately grand mal seizures are infrequent and the most common is the petit mal. This may pass unnoticed during training, or the instructor may see the sufferer behaving oddly over the space of a couple of minutes. If the sufferer is left alone, he will gradually recover his senses and resume training.

Migraine sometimes has a sudden and inexplicable onset and may be so severe as to necessitate abandoning the evening's training. Sometimes the sufferer is unable to find his way home and a friend may have to be sent for. Despite this inconvenience, migraine is no bar to training.

Mentally ill people may well benefit from training. The severe physical exercise and single-minded concentration required seems to ease depression and build confidence. A sympathetic and positive instructor can work wonders with such sufferers. Aggressive students will find the training useful as a safety valve. An evening of supervised and energetic punching and kicking is better than any course of treatment. The modest attainments needed to progress and the recognition of this improvement by the coloured-belt system all lead to a more ordered and healthy mind.

Diabetes sufferers may practise taekwondo as long as they take along a supply of sugar, such as lemonade. The diabetic calculates the activity expected and will adjust his insulin/sugar levels accordingly. Sometimes, however, *joi de vivre* in the training takes over and a little over-exertion causes a drop in blood sugar. This can produce fainting when the level drops too low but, before this, the diabetic may show curious behaviour. The type of behaviour will depend upon the individual but it may well come out as aggression. A little sugar taken at this time will head off any problems.

The Taekwondo Instructor
There is always a risk in teaching people who have a criminal record for violence. To be sure, the sublimation of aggression encountered through taekwondo training is beneficial but there is always the real risk that techniques learned will be used in the street, thereby causing danger to the public and giving taekwondo a bad name.

There is no substitute for the experienced instructor in this instance. He will interview each student and determine their suitability, rather than applying some rigid rule which cannot be expected to apply in all cases. He may well decide to take a chance on the beginner's course, using that time to observe the student and his attitude. A poor performer can be weeded out without having reached the stage of learning potentially dangerous techniques.

Obviously the instructor must have as much information as possible about each student that comes to him. For this reason he will always ask newcomers to fill out an application form that covers the points raised above. When he has this, he can make an initial decision as to whether the applicant is suitable or not. This form will include an application for a Martial Arts Commission licence.

The Martial Arts Commission

The Martial Arts Commission, or MAC as it is generally known, is the Sports Council-recognized controlling body for the martial arts in Britain. It is rather like the British Standards Institute's kitemark which certifies that a product has been rigorously tested and found to measure up. The members of the MAC are all registered martial artists – both students and instructors – and all hold the national MAC licence. This is not a licence as such, since it gives no authority to practise anything, but what it does do is serve as proof of affiliation to the Commission. Instructors' licences are endorsed as such and also carry the name of the martial art in which he is qualified to teach. The practice of WTF Taekwondo in Britain is governed by the British Taekwondo Board (WTF). The Board is responsible for the organisation and development of WTF taekwondo.

The MAC licence also contains a personal insurance that covers the holder in the event of accident and, more importantly, indemnifies him against being sued by third parties. This is especially important since any combat sport involves a real risk of injury, no matter how strictly controlled. The third-party cover guarantees that any person hurt by another taekwondo student has an avenue of financial redress.

The Commission is always mindful of the safety of its practitioners and is the only martial arts organization in Britain to issue personal health record cards. These are small printed cards that slip neatly inside the licence wallet, serving to record any mishap encountered during training or competition. Entries in them are made by the club coach or medical officials. For instance, if a student is knocked out, an entry will be made in his health monitoring card and he will be disbarred from further sparring for at least six weeks.

Membership of the Board also means that complaints

can be followed up and action taken. Although all MAC taekwondo instructors are competent people, complaints can and do arise and the Board is always ready and willing to examine those referred to it. Ultimately the Board is responsible to the Commisssion, so there is no possibility of complaints being swept under the carpet.

Students should be warned that there do exist organizations practising taekwondo which are not MAC registered, but these are not recognized by WTF.

It is a fact, though, that some of the latter can produce large and imposing certificates, covered with authentic-looking Oriental script. One such that was translated by the Commission read 'Two shirts lightly starched; one pair drawers – no starch.' Therefore, if the student decides to join a non-MAC taekwondo club, he is accepting the credentials of the instructor at face value and making his own judgement on the standard of taekwòndo taught there. At best it may only be adequate but it is worth remembering that any qualifications gained will have no standing outside of the organization which confers them. Taekwondo is an Olympic sport and only MAC-recognized taekwondo can give people the chance to represent their country.

The Training Hall

The training hall must be suitable for the practice of taekwondo. This means that the floor should not be stone, concrete or ceramic-tiled. Even a wood block floor can cause injury and there is no doubt that sprung wooden or padded floors are safest. Taekwondo involves a great deal of physical interraction and it is extremely likely that somebody or other is going to hit the deck during an evening's training. When this happens, a padded floor is gratefully acknowledged.

When mats are used, they should be of a type that fit securely together. Mats that move apart can pose a greater risk than a plain floor. There are cases on record where badly fixed mats have trapped and fractured ankles and legs.

The training area must not be overcrowded. During free sparring, a pair of fighters can quickly cover a great deal of ground and too many in a restricted area will lead to people stepping on and falling over one another. Large classes must be staggered, with half the class sitting with feet tucked in at the sides while the other half trains.

Some of the flying kicks used in taekwondo reach a fair height, so low ceilings and light fixtures are definitely out. Pillars can present a serious hazard and, where they are present, they should be effectively padded, especially on the angles. Wall bars must be avoided and loose fittings such as chairs should be moved away from the training area. All bags, shoes and outdoor clothes should be moved from where they can be tripped over. No training should take place near glass doors or low windows. Where these are present, they should be covered with a mesh screen on the inside of the window.

The club instructor must ensure that a good first aid kit is installed and that there are least two qualified first-aiders in the club on any practice night. The location of the nearest hospital with an accident unit must be known and all escape routes from the building should be properly indicated. Taekwondo training generates a great deal of heat and moisture and it is a good idea to have adequate ventilation to clear this away and to reduce slipping on polished floors.

The Training Session
Once the student has received his licence and joined the club, he will begin training after a proper warm-up session. The demanding techniques of taekwondo need a body which is fully prepared and ready to cope with them. This state of readiness is achieved through the warm-up. The normal daily level of activity is very little by comparison to that required for training and so it is necessary to raise the metabolic rate of the body so it can meet the demands to be placed upon it without undue distress or injury. Demand on the heart and lungs must be gradually increased to meet the work-load and so the instructor will take the class through a gradual series of exercises which steadily increase in severity.

The good instructor will not skimp on the warm-up. Once the blood is moving through the muscles at a rate suitable for the work imposed, flexibility work can begin. Taekwondo uses lots of high kicks and these require a fair degree of suppleness. In a powerful kick, the foot is literally thrown high into the air and this can impose intolerable loads on unprepared muscles, tendons and ligaments. Stretching exercises performed passively lengthen muscles and take each joint gently through its maximum range of movement.

Once warm-up is concluded, actual training can begin. Care must be taken when practising powerful but 'unloaded' techniques. These are kicks and punches that are driven out and brought back against no resistance.

It is particularly important that youngsters are not allowed to train wrongly since permanent injury and disfigurement can result. Unloaded techniques should be practised carefully and powerful strikes confined to the punch bag or target mitt.

In pair-form training, the partners should be matched

for size, as far as is possible. A light-boned person practising with a strong student can suffer bad bruising or actual injury even when the latter is controlling his techniques to the best of his ability. Novices must be carefully monitored because they have little control and are apt to land techniques quite heavily on one another. They must be given techniques to practise which are not well beyond their present capabilities and, wherever possible, they should train with higher grades. By this means, the lower grades can practise with a greater degree of safety and the higher grades gain insight into their own knowledge of a technique through teaching it to the novice.

No student should be allowed to free spar until he has a good knowledge of the techniques used and can deliver them without injury against a bag. Competition and sparring together account for the greatest areas of risk in taekwondo and consequently they should be approached sensibly. The partners must have respect for each other and strictly operate a 'do-as-you-would-be-done-by' attitude. The higher-grade or stronger athlete should not use his gift to the disadvantage of his partner but rather to enhance his own safety.

The senior grade should encourage the junior to extend himself, for only by so doing will he learn. Nothing will be learned by a frightened and over-awed partner.

Destruction techniques are a test of power and, like every other part of training, must be approached correctly. Children should not be allowed to break wood or tiles because their young bones can be seriously damaged as a result. For the person who is fascinated by and wishes to develop his breaking efficiency, a course of hand conditioning is necessary. By means of this, the delicate bones of the hand are overlaid with a layer of callous similar to that on the soles of the feet.

Repeated striking of a hard surface can bruise the bones of the hand and lead to an overgrowth of the bone itself. This is not to be recommended since it can affect the fine operation of the fingers. When breaking wood for the first time, care should be taken to choose the right type and ensure it is held rigidly.

At the conclusion of training, it is equally important to cool down and this is done in exactly the same way as the warm-up. Its object is to take the student through a series of exercises which serve as stepping stones between the frenetic activity of the training hall and the more leisurely requirements of everyday life. Failure to operate a good cool-down will certainly result in aches and pains through muscle oedema and lactic acid build-up. Observance of this advice will make the practice of taekwondo safer and more pleasant for all.

CHAPTER 16:
A GLOSSARY OF TERMS USED IN TAEKWONDO

This is a comprehensive glossary of terms used in the various schools of taekwondo. Since the Korean language does not use the English alphabet, transcription causes some slight variations in spelling.

Ageum son	Strike using inside edge of thumb and index finger. Used to attack the throat.
Ahop	Nine.
An-chigi	A strike which travels inwards towards the centre of the opponent's body (*see also* 'Anuro taerigi').
An makgi	Inner block (*see also* 'An marki' and 'An makki') The block is made in an inwards-travelling direction.
An makki	*See above.*
An marki	*See above.*
Annun sogi	A straddle stance, with the back straight, knees bent and feet between 1 and 1½ shoulder-widths apart.
An palja sogi	A ready stance in which the feet are spread and the toes are turned slightly inwards.
Anuro chagi	A general term describing kicks to the knee, calf and lower leg (*see also* 'Noollo chagi' and 'Bakuro chagi').
Anuro makgi	Inward travelling block (*see also* 'Anuro marki').
Anuro marki	*See above.*
Anuro taerigi	*See* 'An chigi'.
Apcha busigi	A front snapping kick which is retrieved as quickly as it is driven out.
Ap-chagi	General term for a front kick.
Ap cha olligi	A blocking technique using the foot.
Apchook	Ball of the foot (*see also* 'Apkumchi').

Ap choomuk	Front fist (*see also* 'Choomuk' and 'Joomeok').
Ape-chigi	A direct strike to the front.
Apjoochom	Short stance with the knees bent and feet splayed.
Apkoobi	Lunge punch delivered with same fist as front foot.
Apkumchi	*See* 'Apchook'.
Ap-makgi	A block used when facing the opponent square on (*see also* 'Ap-marki').
Ap-marki	*See above.*
Apseogi	A short forward stance, with 60/70 percent of body weight on the front foot (*see* 'Ap sogi').
Ap sogi	*See above.*
Ap taerigi	*See* 'Ape-chigi'.
Arae	Lower body and groin (*see also* 'Najunde').
Arae-makki	Lower block (*see also* 'Najunde makgi').
Art	A skill, or application of techniques and method.
Attention stance	A formal ready stance assumed by the student when receiving instruction, or in preparation to begin a practice (*see also* 'Moa seogi' and 'Charyot seogi').
Augment	To strengthen, as in a knife block, by moving both arms in unison, to generate more force, though only one arm actually performs the block (*see also* 'Chung-ga').
Aun no gyo	Breathing exercise in which the student inhales from a low crouching position and then rises to the tips of his toes, with arms extended upwards while exhaling.
Axe kick	A kick in which the straight leg is raised vertically and then dropped heel first onto the opponent. In the dojang, the sole of the foot is used as the impact area.
Back fist	A strike delivered with the tops of the two major knuckles (*see also* 'Dung joomuk', 'Deung joomeok' and 'Yikwon').
Back kick	A kick driven out backwards (*see also* 'Dwi chagi').

Back stance	One in which a large part of the weight rests on the back foot.
Baekjul boolgool	An attitude of confidence and fearlessness when fighting.
Bakat makgi	A block which connects with the outer part of the opponent's arm or leg (see also 'Bakat marki' and Bakkat marki).
Bakat marki	See above.
Bakkat-chigi	An outwards travelling strike (also known as 'Bakuro taerigi').
Bakkat-makki	See 'Bakat makgi'.
Bakuro chagi	See 'Anuro chagi'.
Bakuro makgi	A block which travels from inside to an outwards direction (see also 'Bakuro marki').
Bakuro marki	See above.
Bakuro taerigi	See 'Bakkat chigi'.
Bal	Foot.
Balbadak	Inside edge of foot.
Baldeung	The instep of the foot (see also 'Baldung' and 'Baltung').
Bal dul gi	Lifting the front leg to avoid a sweeping technique.
Baldung	See 'Baldeung' and 'Baltung'.
Bal gurum	Footwork movements.
Balkal	The outer edge of the foot used in some kicks. It is also known as 'Jokdo' and 'Balnal'.
Balkut	The toes.
Balnal	See 'Balkal'.
Baltung	See 'Baldeung'.
Bal twikumchi	Heel of the foot used as an impact area in some kicks.
Bam joomeok	One-knuckle punch.
Bandae chirugi	A punch which is delivered by the same fist as forward leg. Also known as 'Lunge punch', and 'Bandae jireugi'.
Bandae dollyo chagi	A reverse turning kick used against an opponent to the side or rear (see also 'Momdollyo chagi').
Bandae dollyo goro chagi	A reverse hooking kick which moves in the opposite direction to a turning kick.
Bandae jireugi	See 'Bandae chirugi'.
Bandal chagi	A kick in which the sole of the foot sweeps across and into the target. Also known as 'Crescent kick'.

Bandal jireugi	A punch which travels in a semi-circle or full circle.
Bandal son	Reverse knife hand, using base of index finger as impact area.
Bang-au	*See* 'Defence'.
Ban jayoo daeryon	Semi-free sparring, an intermediate between programmed sparring, where every move is pre-planned, and unprogrammed sparring. Fighters take turns as attacker and defender.
Bankyuk	A counter-move to a technique.
Baro jireugi	A punch made with the opposite fist and leg forwards. Also known as 'Reverse punch'.
Batang-son	Palm heel (*see also* 'Chang kwon').
Belt	A cloth strip worn around the waist of the training tunic with colours denoting the degree of competence reached (*see also* 'Ddee').
Beom-seogi	Tiger stance. A form of extreme back stance with nearly all the body weight on the rear leg. The heel of the front foot may be lifted from the ground. Also known as 'Dwit bal sogi'.
Bituro chagi	A twisting kick that travels upwards and around from the inside to the outside.
Black belt	A mark of achievement in practice. There are ten divisions within the black belt known as 'Dan grades'.
Block	A technique used to prevent the opponent's technique from reaching its target.
Bokboo	The stomach area, where life energy is generated (*see also* 'Danjun').
Bong	Wooden staff used by Shaolin monks (*see also* 'Chong bong').
Bow	Formal salutation made by inclining the head and upper body. Also known as 'Kunyeh'.
Breaking	The practice of smashing bricks, tiles and boards to demonstrate the power generated by taekwondo technique. It is known as 'Kyupka'.

Buddhism	A religion which, in one of its aspects, is closely related to the development of taekwondo's ancestor
Butjaba makgi	A block in which the opponent's technique is interrupted and seized. By means of this grasp, the opponent is pulled off balance. It is also called 'Grasping block'.
Butjapgo chagi	A curious single or double leg kick used against a second opponent while the first is being grasped. Also known as 'Japko chagi'.
Centre of gravity	A central point in the body around which the weight is evenly distributed. It is situated approximately at the height of the navel (see 'Choong-sim').
Cha bapgi	A kick which stamps down upon the opponent's instep.
Cha busigi	A collective term for front snap kick, back snap kick, roundhouse kick, reverse turning kick, reverse hook kick and stamping kick.
Chagi	A collective term for all taekwondo kicks.
Cha jireugi	A collective term for back thrust kick ('Dwit -cha jireugi') and side thrust kick ('Youcha jireugi').
Cha mum chagi	A kicking technique used as a block.
Chang-hon Yu	A school of taekwondo founded by General Choi Hong Hi and so called after his pen-name. It is one of three main schools responsible for developing patterns. The school contains twenty patterns of historic and symbolic significance.
Chang kwon	Palm heel, used as an impact area.
Chang mu kwan	An academy of martial arts practice founded by Byun In Yoon during 1946. It refused to become incorporated with General Choi's development of taekwondo.
Charyot seogi	Attention stance with the heels together and feet splayed.

Cheongkwon	Pattern of twenty-seven moves. Title means 'sky'.
Chigi	Collective term for striking techniques.
Chi-jireugi	Uppercut.
Chireugi	A collective term for thrusting. Also known as 'Chirugi', 'Jirugi' or 'Jireugi'.
Chirugi	*See above.*
Chodan	Black belt first dan.
Choi-yong	A pattern named after a famous fourteenth-century Korean military commander and consisting of forty-five movements.
Chojum	The point at which maximum energy of a technique is focused for maximal effect (*see* 'Focus').
Choke	A technique which restricts breathing or blood circulation to the brain.
Chong Bong	The six-foot staff (*see also* 'Bong').
Chongul	A forward stance with equal weight distribution over both legs.
Chon-ji	Pattern named after the creation of humanity.
Chookyo makgi	A head block intended to deflect a downwards travelling blow (*see also* 'Chukyo marki').
Choomuk	*See* 'Ap choomuk'.
Choongdan	The mid-section of the body, from base of the neck to waist.
Choong-jang	Pattern named after the pseudonym of a fifteenth-century Korean general *see also* 'Chung-jang').
Choong-moo	Pattern named after the reputed inventor of the armoured warship (*see also* 'Chung-mu').
Choong-sim	Centre of gravity.
Chop	A blocking or striking technique using the little finger-side of the palm.
Chukyo marki	*See* 'Chookyo makgi'.
Chung do kwan	A martial art academy founded by Won Kook Lee in 1945.
Chung-ga	*See* 'Augment'.
Chung-gun	Pattern named after a nineteenth-century Korean patriot.

Chung-jang	*See* 'Choong-jang'.
Chung-mu	*See* 'Choong-moo'.
Chwa	Left.
Circular block	A blocking technique which redirects the energy of an attack by means of a circular movement. It is known as a 'Dolli myo makgi'.
Circular movements	Moves which do not proceed in a straight line but describe a circular path during usage.
Close-range techniques	Techniques which can generate force over a short distance.
Close stance	A formal, feet-together stance (*see also* 'Moa seogi').
Combination	Series of techniques performed consecutively or concurrently, or a combination of the two (*see* 'Yonsok').
Control	The regulation of force and impact so that injury is minimized.
Coordination	Generation of correct sequences of action, producing a smooth and progressive movement.
Counter	A technique used in response to another (*see also* 'Bankyuk').
Crane stance	*See* 'Haktari segoi' and 'Hanbal sogi'.
Crescent kick	*See* 'Bandal chagi'.
Crescent punch	*See* 'Bandal jireugi'.
Daebee	Guard. The position of the hands and body so attacks and counters can be mounted with minimum risk.
Daebee marki	Block using both hands in front of the chest.
Daeryon	Collective word for the various forms of sparring.
Dallyon joo	Punching post used to condition the striking surfaces of the hands and feet.
Dan-gun	Pattern named after the legendary founder of Korea.
Danjun	The centre of life-energy generation within the body (*see also* 'Bokboo').
Danjun ki	Breathing exercise assisting the generation of life energy.
Dari	Leg
Dari pyogi	Leg flexibility exercises.
Ddee	The belt.

Dduiyo chagi	General term for a jumping kick (*see also* 'Deemyun chagi').
Dee jeea jireugi	A short double or single punch used as a close-range technique.
Deemyun bandae dollyo chagi	A flying reverse turning kick in which the body rotates through 360 degrees. Also known as the 'Twimyo bandae dollyo chagi'.
Deemyun bituro chagi	A flying twisting kick performed to the front and also known as 'Twimyo bituro chagi'.
Deemyun chagi	A collective term of flying kicks. Also known as 'Twimyo chagi' or 'Twieo chagi'.
Deemyun dollyo chagi	Flying turning kick. Also known as 'Twimyo dollyo chagi'.
Deemyun ijung yop chagi	Flying double kick which attacks two targets from an airborne position. Also known as 'Twimyo ijung yop chagi'.
Deemyun yopcha jireugi	A flying sidekick in which the body rotates sideways on delivery. Also known as 'Twimyo yopcha jireugi'.
Defence	Tactics used to protect against attack.
Deflect	To redirect, rather than halt, an incoming technique.
Deung joomeok	Back fist.
Diagonal stance	A form of straddle stance in which the feet are twice shoulder-width apart (*see also* 'Sasun sogi').
Digutja chireugi	A sideways travelling double punch, using one fist to attack the face and the other the body. Also known as 'U-punch'.
Distraction	A feint used during free sparring to divert the opponent's attention away from a course of intended action.
Dobok	Taekwondo training uniform. It is white in colour but may have coloured stripes along edges.
Dojang	Training hall.
Dolgi	Turning.
Dolli myo makgi	*See* 'Circular block'.
Dollyo chagi	Turning kick which uses a combination of hip-swivel and knee action to drive the kick out in a circular path (*see also* 'Tolyo chagi').

Dollyo jireugi	Turning punch which travels from the hip in a semi-circular direction.
Doobaldangsang	Flying kick using both feet to hit the same target.
Dool	Two.
Doo Palmok	An augmented forearm block.
Doo Sankarak chireugi	Two-finger spear hand used to attack the eyes.
Dora	Formal command to perform a turn.
Doro chagi	A deflecting technique using the foot to redirect a low attack.
Dosan	Taekwondo pattern of twenty-four movements.
Double block	A concurrent technique designed to stop two simultaneous attacks.
Double kick	A concurrent delivery of two kicks to different targets or a consecutive delivery using one leg (*see* 'Yichoong chagi').
Double punch	A concurrent or consecutive delivery of two punches to different targets.
Double block	A concurrent or consecutive usage of two blocks in response to two techniques (*see* 'Yichoong marki).
Downward block	A technique designed to block attacks to the lower part of the body. Known as 'Naeryo marki'.
Dung joomeok	*See* 'Back fist' and 'Yikwon'.
Dung sonkal	Reverse knife hand, using the area at the base of the index finger, on the thumb-side of the palm, as impact area.
Dung sonmok	A block using the wrist.
Duro marki	A scooping block that catches and lifts an attack.
Dwi chagi	General term for 'Back kick'.
Dwichook	The bottom of the heel.
Dwikoomchi	The rear of the heel.
Dwiro-chigi	Elbow strike delivered to someone standing behind.
Dwit bal sogi	*See* 'Beom seogi'.
Dwitcha busigi	Back kick which quickly retrieves kicking leg after use.
Dwitcha jireugi	Back thrusting kick.
Dwit koaseogi	An x-stance where the calf of one leg wedges the shin of the other. Also known as 'Koa seogi'.

Dwitkoobi	Back stance in which the front and rear feet are flat on the floor at 90 degrees to each other and the majority of weight is on the rear foot. Also known as 'Niunja sogi'.
Edge of foot	The outer edge of the foot used in kicking techniques. It is known as 'Balnal' or 'Balkal'.
Edge of hand	The thumb- or little finger-edge of the hand used in striking techniques. It is known as 'Sonkal'.
Elbow	Used in various ways as a close quarter weapon and known as 'Palkoop' or 'Palkumchi'.
Eolgool	Face.
Eolgool makki	Face block.
Eotgeoreo makki	X-block, using both of the forearms. It is also known as 'Gyocha joomuk'.
Eui am	Pattern of forty-five moves.
Fist	Made by rolling the fingers into the palm. A common weapon typically using the knuckles of the index and middle finger as impact areas (*see* 'Ap choomuk').
Flying back kick	Flying kick using the heel of the foot while the body leans away.
Flying crescent kick	Flying kick using the inner edge or sole of the foot.
Flying double side kick	Flying double kick which attacks two targets before landing. Also known as 'Twimyo ijung yop chagi'.
Flying front kick	Flying snap kick to the front (*see* 'Goolleo chagi').
Flying kick	Collective term for any kick delivered while both feet are off the ground. Also known as 'Twimyo chagi', 'Twieo chagi' or 'Deemyun chagi'.
Flying reverse turning kick	*See* 'Deemyun bandae dollyo chagi' or 'Twimyo bandae dollyo chagi'.
Flying turning kick	*See* 'Deemyun dollyo chagi' or 'Twimyo dollyo chagi'.
Flying side kick	*See* 'Deemyun yopcha jireugi' or 'Twimyo yopcha jireugi'.
Flying twisting kick	*See* 'Deemyun bituro chagi' or 'Twimyo bituro chagi'.

Focus	*See* 'Chojum'.
Follow-through	Continuation of a technique to completion.
Follow-up	A consecutive technique in a combination.
Forearm	Blocking area of the arm, known as 'Palmok'.
Forward stance	A long forward-facing stance with a bent front knee and a straight back leg.
Free-style sparring	Unprogrammed sparring where the opponents exchange techniques freely but use control. Known as 'Jayoo daeryon'.
Front block	*See* 'Apmakgi'.
Front kick	A straight kick directed towards the front and impacting with the ball of the foot or the heel/sole.
Fugul	A back stance with 70 percent of body weight on the rear foot.
Gawison-keut	Two-finger spear hand.
Geuman	Conclusion.
Gi	Life energy
Golcho chagi	Hooking kick used against the opponent's knee or elbow.
Golcho makgi	Hooking block used to trap the opponent's techniques.
Goman	Command to stop.
Gomson	Semi-closed hand used as a weapon.
Gong gyuk	Attack.
Gong gyuk gi	Attacking techniques.
Goolleo chagi	Flying front kick.
Goro chagi	Sweeping kick used to unbalance the opponent.
Goyanghee sogi	Tiger stance in which 90 percent of body weight is on the rear foot.
Grading	An examination of competence.
Grasping block	*See* 'Butjaba makgi'.
Guard	Relationship of hands and feet giving a good possibility for attack and defence.
Gujari dolgi	Turning on the spot to meet an attacker.
Gungul sogi	'Walking stance' in which the front foot faces fowards and the rear turns 25 degrees outwards.
Gun shin pup	Ancient Korean techniques of stealth.
Gup	Grades of proficiency below black-belt level.
Gwang-gae	A pattern.

Gyocha joomuk	*See* 'Eotgeoreo makki'.
Gyohari-seogi	Short, knees-bent stance.
Ha'i	Training trousers.
Haktari-seogi	One-legged stance, the other foot resting on the supporting knee. Also known as 'Crane stance' or 'Hanbal sogi'.
Hammer fist	Little finger-side of the closed fist used as a block against kicks. Also known as 'Mitchoomuk' or 'Me-joomeok'.
Hana	One
Hanbal sogi	*See* 'Haktari-seogi'.
Han mu kwan	Korean martial art school.
Han songarak chirugi	One-finger strike used to attack the eyes and throat.
Hansoo	Pattern of twenty-seven moves. The title means 'water'.
Hapkido	Korean fighting system using locks, holds and throws.
Hardan	Part of the body below the belt.
Hardan kyocha	Downward-directed x-block.
Hardan marki	Downward block.
Hauri	Hip
Hechyo makki	Double block using an outwards movement of both forearms.
Heel kick	Any kick using the heel as the impact area.
Himm	Force or power.
Ho-goo	Protective equipment worn while sparring.
Hohoop	Breathing.
Hohup chojul	Breath control as a means of harnessing power.
Hooking block	*See* 'Golcho makgi'.
Hooking kick	*See* 'Golcho chagi'.
Hook punch	Close-range technique curving during delivery.
Hooryo chagi	A turning kick which continues on through.
Horse stance	Also known as 'Straddle stance'. The legs are separated widely and the back is straight (*see* 'Kima-sogi').
Hosin sul	Self-defence techniques.
Hullyo marki	Block using the arms which draws the opponent off balance.
Hwa rang	The 'flowering youth'. A name given to a warrior army of ancient Korea.
Hwa rang do	The Hwa rang's ethics and techniques

Hyung	Pattern. Otherwise known as 'Poomse'. It is a series of movements and techniques.
Ilbo daeryon	One-step sparring.
Ilgope	Seven.
Ilgup	First class, as in a grading standard.
Ill	First.
Ilyo	Pattern of twenty-seven moves. The title means 'oneness'.
Inji choomuk	Semi-open fist, impacting with the middle knuckles (*see also* 'Pyon joomeok').
Instep	*See* 'Baldeung'.
Jajeunbal	*See* 'Jajun bal'.
Jajun bal	The use of footwork to dodge a technique.
Japko chagi	*See* 'Butjapgo chagi'.
Jayoo daerion	*See* 'Free sparring'.
Jeja	Student.
Ji do kwan	Korean martial arts school.
Jip joong	Concentration.
Jiptjung	Harmonizing the internal with the external through breathing.
Jireugi	General term for striking.
Jirumyo chagi	Airborne combination of a kick with a punch.
Jitae ·	Pattern of twenty-eight moves. The word means 'earth'.
Jokdo	Edge of the foot.
Jok gi	Foot techniques.
Jokgi daeryon	Pre-arranged sparring using foot techniques.
Joochoomseogi	A high straddle stance.
Joomeok	Fist (*see also* 'Joomuk').
Joomuk	*See above*.
Joonbi	*See* 'Junbi'.
Joong bong	Middle-sized staff.
Junbi	Ready.
Junbi sogi	Ready stance.
Kae-baek	Pattern named after seventh-century general.
Kakup	Rank.
Kang duk. won	Early Korean martial arts.
Keumgang	Pattern of twenty-seven moves. Title means 'diamond'.
Keupso chirigi	Art of attacking the body's vital points.
Kihap	Shout.
Kima sogi	Horseriding stance.
Knee	Close quarters weapon known as 'Mooreup'.

Knife hand	A strike delivered with the little finger-side of the hand (*see* 'Sudo').
Koa-seogi	*See* 'Dwit koaseogi'.
Ko dang	Pattern named after Korean patriot.
Kong soo do	Korean fighting system heavily influenced by Japanese karate. Means 'empty hand way'.
Koodan	Ninth-degree black belt.
Koryo	Dynasty of Korea from AD 918 – 1392. Also name of a pattern with twenty-seven moves.
Kup	*See* 'Gup'.
Kupso	The vital points on the body.
Kwonbop	Chinese system of unarmed combat adopted in Korea. Also known as 'Kwonpup'.
Kwonpup	*See above.*
Kyocha marki	Cross block.
Kyokpa	Breaking techniques (*see also* 'Kyupka').
Kyungye	A command to bow.
Kyupka	*See* 'Kyokpa'.
L-stance	*See* 'Dwitkoobi' and 'Niunja-sogi'.
Lunge punch	Punch with same leading fist as leg (*see* 'Bandae chireugi').
Makgi	General term for blocks (*see also* 'Marki').
Marki	*See above.*
Martial	Military, or pertaining to war.
Martial arts	Military techniques and systems.
Mikeureumbal	Shifting the body by moving both feet.
Mikulgi	Moving by sliding the feet.
Miro makgi	A pushing block using the forearms or palms of the hands to unbalance an opponent. Also known as 'Miro marki'.
Mit-choomuk	Hammer fist (*see also* 'Yaup choomuk' and 'Me joomeok').
Mo seogi	One foot slightly leading the other.
Moa sogi	Basic, feet-together stance.
Modeumbal	Drawing the feet together.
Modeumbal-chagi	Flying kick where both feet strike the target.
Mojoochoom	Form of straddle stance with one foot slightly advanced.
Mokpyo	Targets on head or body for landing blows.

Mom	The body.
Momchau makgi	A form of strengthened block using two forearms.
Momdollyo-chagi	Spinning back kick (*see* 'Bandae dollyo chagi').
Momtong	Trunk of body.
Momtong an-makki	Blocking to mid-section with the same fist and leg leading.
Momtong makki	General term for mid-section blocks.
Moo duk kwan	A school of Korean martial art.
Moon-moo	Pattern.
Mooreup	Knee.
Mo-seogi	A stance in which one foot is placed forward.
Myung chi	Solar plexus.
Nachugi	Body evasion through ducking.
Naeryo-chigi	Downwards-travelling punch.
Naeryo jireugi	Downwards-travelling thrust.
Naeryo marki	Downwards-travelling block.
Najunde	Lower part of the body; below the belt.
Narani sogi	A ready stance in preparation for practice.
Neikya	Fighting system developed from Kwonbop.
Net	Four
Niunja sogi	*See* 'L-stance'.
Noollo chagi	*See* 'Anuro chagi'.
Noollo makgi	*See* 'Anuro makgi'.
Nop chagi	Flying kick using both feet to impact.
Nopunde	Upper body, including head.
Nopunde makgi	High block.
Oh	Five.
Ohdan	Fifth dan.
Olly o-chigi	An upwards-travelling elbow strike.
Omgyo didigi	Covering a long distance by stepping.
Omyo mikulgi	Covering distance by sliding the feet over the ground.
One knuckle fist	A hand weapon using the extended middle knuckle of the index or middle finger (*see* 'Bam joomeuk').
One leg stance	*See* 'Crane stance', 'Haktari seogi' and 'Hanbal sogi'.
One step sparring	Pair-form practice where a technique is responded to immediately it is delivered.
Orun	Right.

Pachigi	Korean martial art using head butts.
Pal	Eight. Also means 'Arms'.
Paldan	Eight-dan black belt.
Palgwe	Series of patterns based upon the eight trigrams of the I'Ching.
Palkoop	*See* 'Elbow' and 'Palkumchi'.
Palkoop-chigi	Elbow strike.
Palkumchi	*See* 'Palkoop'.
Palm heel	Base of the palm used as a strike or block (*see* 'Chang kwon' and 'Batang-son').
Palmok	Forearm or wrist.
Parro	Return, i.e., to ready stance.
Parry	To deflect or block an attack.
Pattern	A training system consisting of a series of a whole series of pre-arranged moves in a continuous sequence (*see also* 'Poomse' and 'Hyung').
Phihagi	Use of footwork in dodging techniques.
Poomse	*See* 'Pattern' and 'Hyung'.
Po-un	Pattern named after Korean poet.
Pre-arranged sparring	Pair-form practice with the attack and defence agreed in advance.
Pyongwon	Pattern of thirty-one moves. Title means 'plain'.
Pyon joomeok	Half-open fist.
Pyonson-keut	Spear hand
Pyonson-keut sewochireugi	Spear hand thrust to solar plexus made with thumb upwards.
Pyonson-keut eopeochireugi	As above, both with palm facing downwards.
Pyugi	Stretching.
Range	The distance, as for a technique.
Rank	Level of proficiency held. Coloured belts denote rank.
Ready stance	A stance assumed in preparation for practice or at conclusion of practice.
Recoil	The reaction produced upon impact.
Referee	Official conducting a competition.
Reflex action	Automatic reaction to a stimulus.
Reverse punch	Punch using the opposite arm to the forward leg (*see* 'Baro chireugi').

Reverse turning kick	Turning kick impacting with the heel or sole of foot.
Reverse knife hand	*See* 'Dung sonkal' and 'Yok sudo'.
Sa	Four.
Sabom	Teacher or instructor (*see also* 'Sabum', 'Sah bom' and 'Sabumnim').
Sabum	*See above.*
Sabumnim	*See above.*
Sadan	Fourth-dan black belt.
Sah bom	*See* 'Sabom'.
Salutation	Formal greeting.
Sam	Three.
Sambo daeryon	Three-step sparring with the defence technique employed on the third consecutive attack.
Samdan	Third-dan black belt.
Sam-il	Pattern of thirty-three movements.
Sandan marki	Upward block.
Sangdan	Face and head area.
Sangdan marki	*See* 'Sandan marki'.
Sangdan kyocha marki	X-block to head attack.
Sasun sogi	*See* 'Diagonal stance'.
Se-jong	Pattern of twenty-four movements named after a Korean King.
Semi-free sparring	*See* 'Ban jayoo daeryon'.
Set	Three. Also used as alternative term for 'Pattern'.
Sewao-jireugi	Vertical punch delivered with the thumb uppermost. Also known as 'Sewo chireugi'.
Sewo chireugi	*See above.*
Shejak	Command meaning 'Begin'.
Shib	Tenth.
Shibum	Demonstration.
Shihap	Bout or match.
Side kick	Straight kick delivered with the heel (*see* 'Yop chagi'). Side snap kick is a jabbing kick whereas side thrust kick is a powerful, penetrating technique.
Simsa	Grading test.
Sipdan	Tenth-dan black belt.
Sipjin	Pattern of thirty-one moves. Title means 'decimal'.
Snap	Method of execution of punch, kick or strike in which the limb is whip-lashed out and back.

Sogi	General term for stance or position.
Sokdo	Speed.
Sokim	Feint.
Sole of foot	Impact area of the body.
Sonbadak	Palm.
Sondung	Back fist (see also 'Deung joomeok').
Sondung mok marki	Block using the bent wrist.
Sonkal	Knife hand (see also 'Sonnal').
Sonnal	See above.
Sonnal deung	Reverse knife hand.
Sonnal makki	Knife block.
Soobahk	Twelfth-century Korean fighting art (see also 'Subak').
Soopyung chireugi	Horizontal double punch to the side of the body. One arm is straight and the other sharply bent.
Sooryon	Training.
Sparring	Pair-form practice of a programmed or unprogrammed nature.
Spear hand	Impact technique using the fingertips.
Spinning kicks	Those kicks which use a 180 or 360 degree rotation of the body during delivery.
Stamping kick	A downwards-travelling kick, impacting with the heel.
Subak	See 'Soobahk'.
Sudo	Knife hand strike (see 'Knife hand').
Sweep	Foot technique which breaks the opponent's balance (see 'Goro chagi').
Taebaek	Pattern of twenty-six moves.
Taegeuk	Series of eight basic patterns.
Tae kyon	Ancient Korean fighting art used by peasants. Also known as 'Taekyun'.
Taekyun	See above.
Taekwondo	'Foot/fist art' adopted by Korean martial art Masters in 1955. Umbrella title for traditional and modern Korean systems.
Taesudo	Original name for modern and ancient Korean martial arts/ combat sports. Replaced by taekwondo.
Take-down	Technique which deposits the opponent on the floor.

Tang soo do	'Art of the China hand'. Korean fighting system influenced by Japanese karate.
Tasut	Five.
Tiger stance	*see* 'Goyanghee sogi'
Toi-gye	Pattern named after sixteenth-century scholar.
Tolyo chagi	*See* 'Turning kick' and 'Dollyo chagi'.
Tong-il	Pattern.
To-san	Pattern named after Korean patriot.
Turning kick	Circular kick impacting with the ball or sole of foot (*see* 'Tolyo chagi').
Turning punch	Punch describing a wide, circling path.
Twichibo chireugi	Punch, most often an uppercut, delivered with the palm uppermost (*see also* 'Chi-jireugi').
Twieo-chagi	General term for flying or jumping kick.
Twisting kick	Kick in which the striking area rotates slightly to accommodate the opponent's angle.
Ul-ji	Pattern named after a Korean general.
Umji choomuk	A punch delivered with the thumb joint.
Undong	Exercise.
Uppercut	Punch travelling in an upwards direction (*see* 'Twichibo chireugi' and 'Chi-jireugi').
U-punch	*See* 'Digutja chireugi'.
Upward block	*See* 'Sandan marki' and 'Sangdan kyocha marki'
Vertical punch	One in which the thumb is uppermost (*see* 'Sewao-jireugi').
Vital points	Areas of vulnerability on the body.
Weikya	Korean fighting system developed from Kwonbop.
Wheel kick	Spinning kick in which the body rotates 180 degrees during delivery.
Won-hyo	Pattern named after a Buddhist monk.
X-block	Block where one forearm overlays the other (*see* 'Kyocha marki').
Yaksok daeryon	Pre-arranged sparring.

Yaudal	Eight.
Yaul	Ten.
Yaup choomuk	Hammer fist (*see also* 'Mit choomuk').
Yausut	Six.
Yeebo daeryon	Two-step sparring, with the defence made on the second consecutive attack.
Yeop chagi	Side kick (*see also* 'Yop chagi').
Yeop makki	Side block (*see also* 'Yop marki').
Yeopeuro chigi	Horizontal elbow strike.
Yichoong chagi	Double kick.
Yichoong marki	Double block.
Yidan	Second-dan black belt.
Yikwon	Back fist (*see also* 'Sondung').
Yok sudo	Reverse knife hand (*see also* 'Dung sonkal').
Yonsok	Combination.
Yookdan	Sixth-dan black belt.
Yop jireugi	Sideways punch.
Yop chagi	Side kick (*see* 'Yeop chagi').
Yop marki	Side block (*see* 'Yeop makki').
Yul-kok	Pattern with thirty-eight movements.
Yu-sin	Pattern with sixty-eight movements.

BASIC TAEGEUKS FOR PRACTICE
Taegeuk 1

START   2   3   4

9   10   11   12

17   18   19   20

5   6   7   8

13   14   15   16

21   FINISH

Taegeuk 2

START   2   3   4

9   10   11   12

17   18   19   20   21

5

6

7

8

13

14

15

16

22

23

24

FINISH

Taegeuk 3

START

2

3

4

9

10

11

12

17

18

19

20

25

26

27

28

29

5

6

7

8

13

14

15

16

21

22

23

24

30

31

32

33

34

35

FINISH

Taegeuk 4

START 2 3 4

9 10 11 12 13

18 19 20 21 22

27 28 29 30 FINISH

5   6   7   8

14   15   16   17

23   24   25   26

Taegeuk 5

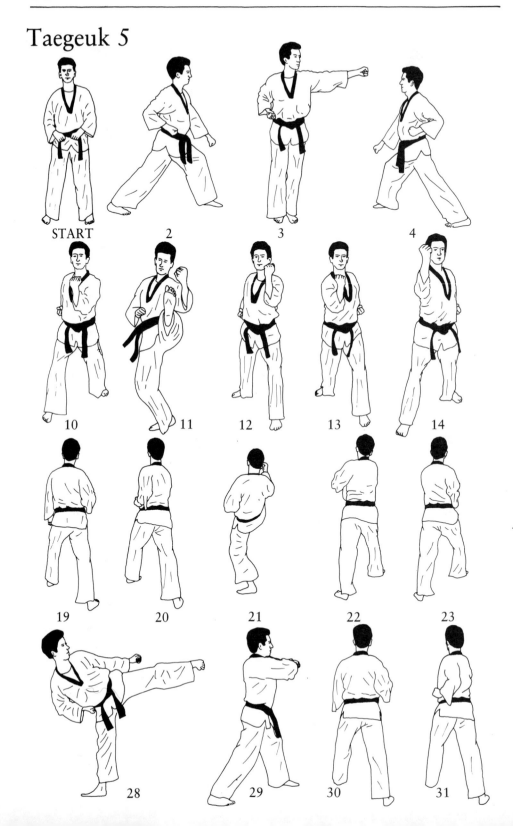

START   2   3   4

10   11   12   13   14

19   20   21   22   23

28   29   30   31

5   6   7   8   9

15   16   17   18

24   25   26   27

32   33   FINISH

Taegeuk 6

START

2

3

4

9

10

11

12

17

18

19·

20

25

26

27

28

5

6

7

8

13

14

15

16

21

22

23

24

29

30

31

32

FINISH

Taegeuk 7

START

2

3

4

10

11

12

13

14

20

21

22

23

29

30

31

32

33

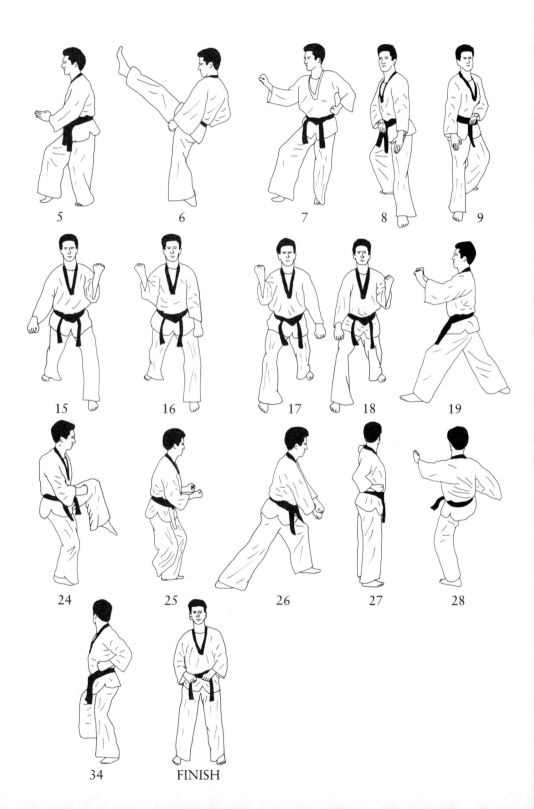

5

6

7

8

9

15

16

17

18

19

24

25

26

27

28

34

FINISH

Taegeuk 8

START 2 3 4 5 6 7

12 13 14 15 16 17

22 23 24 25

32 33 34 35

8   9   10   11

18   19   20   21

26   27   28   29   30   31

36   37   38   FINISH

ACKNOWLEDGEMENTS

I would like to acknowledge the contribution of the following persons without whose help this book could not have been written:

President Un Yong Kim of the Kukkiwon, Seoul, for information on the World Taekwondo Federation given during a fact-finding visit in 1978.

The British Taekwondo Board of Control (WTF) for their kind assistance in the preparation of this book.

John Ingram and Thomas MacCullum for their patience and the invaluable assistance they provided during the final editing.

Kang Uk Lee for his fascinating 'I was there' insights into the setting up of the Korean Taesoodo and Taekwondo Associations.

Ki Ha Rhee O. C. M. for several invaluable seminars on the origin and practices of taekwondo. Thanks also for supplying me with his personal copy of *Taekwon-Do* by General Choi Hong Hi.

Con Halpin, second dan of the British Taekwondo Board of Control (WTF), for the many hours he spent explaining patterns, techniques and grading systems used within the WTF and for posing for the photographs used in this book.

Kevin Woollett, first dan of the BTBC, for demonstrating some of the techniques depicted.

Dr Jim Canney for his work towards making the practice of martial arts safer for all to practise.

Rex Hazeldine of Loughborough College for advice on fitness and training routines.

Tony Gummerson of Leeds University for explaining the importance of correct coaching.

INDEX

advancing stance, 27
aerobic fitness, 121–2
aggression, 139
aikido, 8
anaerobic fitness, 122–3
arms: blocking techniques, 61–2, 69; as weapons, 19; see also hands; punches
asthma, 138
attention stance, 24, Fig. 6
attitude, mental, 10–12
axe kick, 52, Fig. 68

back arches, 128
back exercises, 135
back fist, 31–2, Figs. 18, 19, 133
back kick, 39, 48–51, 74–6, Figs. 38, 65–7, 118, 119, 124, 140, 143; flying back kick, 57, Figs. 81–4
back stance, 26–7, 28, 29, Fig. 11
balance, 72
basic techniques, 40–57, Figs. 39–85
belts, grading system, 11, 15
blocking techniques, 32, 58–69 , Figs. 92–110; blocking kicks, 67–9, Figs. 108–10; combination techhniques, 71–2
body armour, 14, 98, 102, 107
body positioning, free sparring, 103
body weapons, 16–17, 30–9, Figs. 17–38
bone callouses, 115, 143
bouts, competitions, 109–10
bow, standing, 12, Fig. 1
boxes, 14
brain damage, 19, 120
breaking, see destruction training
breathing, 19–20; pattern training, 82
breathlessness, 138
bricks, destruction techniques, 115–17
brieze blocks, destruction techniques, 115–16, 118
British Taekwondo Board TF), 140–1
burpees, 128, Figs. 156–60

callouses, 114–15, 143
chang hun, 8
Changmu Kwan, 8
children: destruction training, 120, 143; press-ups, 126; safety, 142

Choi-yong pattern, 82
Chon-ji pattern, 82
Choong-jang pattern, 82
Choong-moo pattern, 82
Chungdo Kwan, 8
circuit training, 122–3
closed stance, 24
clothing, competitions, 107
coaches, 10, 100–1, 113, 139–40
combination techniques, 13, 70–9, Figs. 111–29; patterns, 81–5, 86
competition taekwondo, 106–13; free sparring, 14
competitiveness, free sparring, 100
conditioning: body weapons, 30; hands and feet, 114–15, 143
controlled contact, free sparring, 14
cooling-down exercises, 143
courage, 11
crane stance, 27
crescent kick, 39, 52, 62, Figs. 37, 69–71, 141; flying reverse crescent kick, 57, Fig. 85; reverse crescent kick, 52, 79, Figs. 72–4, 128

Dan-gun pattern, 82
deflection, 60–1
destruction techniques, 14–15, 114–20; safety, 143
developing force, 16–22
diabetes, 139
Do-san pattern, 82
dojang, 12
double blocks, 66
drug tests, competitions, 108

elbow: blocking techniques, 61–2; strikes, 18, 35–7, Figs. 29–33, 137
epilepsy, 138–9
Eui-am pattern, 82–3
evasion, 58–9; pre-arranged sparring, 88–9
exercises, physical fitness, 121–35, Figs. 152–70
eyes, in pre-arranged sparring, 89

face, safety, 98
feet: blocking techniques, 62; conditioning, 114–15; as weapons, 19, 30, 38–9, Figs. 35–8; see also kicks
feints, 71, 103
fighting stance, 24, 29, Figs. 9, 116, 120, 125
fingers, as weapons, 34–5, Fig. 28; see also fists; hands

fireman's lift, 130
fists, 19, 30–2; back fist, 31–2, Figs. 18, 19, 133; hammer fist, 32, 118–19, Fig. 20; horizontal back fist, 31, Figs. 18, 19; upright back fist, 31
fitness, 121–35
flexibility exercises, 123–4, 142
floors: competition areas, 106; safety, 141
flying back kick, 57, Figs. 81–4
flying front kick, 54
flying kicks, 54–7, Figs. 76–85
flying reverse crescent kick, 57, Fig. 85
flying side kick, 54, Figs. 78–80
flying turning kick, 54, Figs. 76, 77
force, developing, 16–22
forearm blocks, 69
forearm guards, 14, 107
forms, see patterns
forward stance, 24, 26, 29, Figs. 10, 14
free sparring, 14–15, 88, 98–105; safety, 143
front kick, 17, 38, 43–5, 74, 104–5, 120, Figs. 42–8, 111–14; flying front kick, 54
front snap kick, 21

Ge-Baek pattern, 83
grading system, 10–11, 15
groin guards, 107
gumshields, 14, 107

haemophilia, 138
half-point penalties, competitions, 112–13
hammmer block, 67
hammer fist, 32, 118–19, Fig. 20
hands: blocking techniques, 61; conditioning, 114–15, 143; weapons, 30–5, Figs. 17–28; see also fists; punches
Hansoo pattern, 83
hapkido, 9
head, safety, 19
head butt, 120
heart, fitness, 121–2, 137–8
heart disease, 137–8
high-energy punches, 19–21
hips: flexibility, 131; stretching exercises, 133
history of taekwondo, 8–9
horizontal back fist, 31, Figs. 18, 19
horizontal strike, 32
hourglass stance, 28
Hwa-rang pattern, 83

ice, destruction techniques, 115, 117

I'Ching, 84, 85
illness and taekwondo training, 138–9
Ilyo pattern, 83
impact energy, 16, 18–19, 30
impact pads, 14
injuries, competitions, 111–12
inner block, 65–6, Figs. 96–9, 135
instep, as a weapon, 18, Fig. 34
instructors, 10, 100–1, 113, 139–40
insurance, 140
International Olympic Committee (IOC), 108

jabs, 42, 73–4, Figs. 126, 149
Jido Kwan, 8
Jitae pattern, 83
joints: stretching exercises, 124; suppleness exercises, 123
Joong-gun pattern, 83
judges, competitions, 106–7, 108
judo, 8
jury, competitions, 106–7, 108

karate, 8, 114
kendo, 8
Keumgang pattern, 83
kicks, 18, 21–2; axe kick, 52, Fig. 68; back kick, 39, 48–51, 74–6, Figs. 38, 65–7, 118, 119, 124, 140, 143; blocking kicks, 67–9, Figs. 108–10; combination techniques, 73, 74–9, Figs. 111–15; competitions, 110–11; crescent kick, 39, 52, 62, Figs. 37, 69–71, 141; destruction techniques, 114; flying kicks, 54–7, Figs. 76–85; free sparring, 104–5; front kick, 17, 38, 43–5, 74, 104–5, 120, Figs. 42–8, 111–14; front snap kick, 21; one-step side kick, 48; one-step turning kick, 46–8, Figs. 52–4; reverse crescent kick, 52, 79, Figs. 72–4, Fig. 128; reverse turning kick, 39, 52–4, 74, 105, Fig. 75; safety, 142; side kick, 48, 105, Figs. 55–64, 138; side snap kick, 38; side thrust kick, 21–2, 38–9, Figs. 5, 36; thrusting front kick, 44; turning kick, 22, 45–8, 59, 70–1, 72, 74–6, 79, 104–5, Figs. 49–54, 115, 129–30, 146, 151
kinetic energy, 17, 18, 19
knee: blocking techniques, 62;

exercises, 130; as a weapon, 37–8
knife block, 61, 62–5, Figs. 90–5
knife hand, 33–4, 119–20, Figs. 22–5, 136
knock-downs, competitions, 111
knock-outs, competitions, 111–12
knuckles: callouses, 115; one-knuckle punch, 32; press-ups, 126; *see also* fists
Ko-dang pattern, 83
Korea, martial arts, 7–9
Korean Taekwondo Association, 8–9
Korean Taesoodo Association, 8
Koryo pattern, 83–4
Kwang-gae pattern, 84

lactic acid, 121–2, 143
legs: exercises, 130–5, Figs. 161–70; as weapons, 19; *see also* kicks
ligaments, 123
lunge punch, 17–18, 40–2, 70, Figs. 39–41
lungs, fitness, 122, 137, 138

Martial Arts Commission (MAC), 140–1
mats, 106, 141
menstrual cycle, 101
mental attitude, 10–12
mental illness, 139
migraine, 139
mirrors, practice with, 72, 101–2
Mooduk Kwan, 8
Moon-moo pattern, 84
motivation, free sparring, 98–100
mouthguards, 14, 107
multi-step sparring, 13
muscles: aerobic fitness, 121–2; anaerobic fitness, 122–3; high-energy punches, 19–20; stretching exercises, 123–4, 142; warming-up exercises, 13

natural stance, 25
neck exercises, 135

one-armed press-ups, 126
one-knuckle punch, 32
one-step side kick, 48
one-step sparring, 13, 90–7, Figs. 131–51
one-step turning kick, 46–8, Figs. 52–4
outer block, 66–7, Figs. 100–7
oxygen, aerobic fitness, 121–2

pair-form sparring, 12, 13
pair-form training, safety, 142–3
Palgwe pattern, 84
palm: blocking techniques, 61; palm heel, 33, Fig. 21
patterns, 13, 81–5, 86
penalties, competitions, 112–13
physical fitness, 121–35
Po-eun pattern, 84
pre-arranged sparring, 72, 86–7, Figs. 131–51
press-ups, 125–6, Figs. 152–3
pressing blocks, 61
proprioceptors, 123–4
punches, 17, 19; combination techniques, 70–4; destruction techniques, 114; high-energy, 19–21; lunge punch, 17–18, 40–2, 70, Figs. 39–41; one-knuckle punch, 32; reverse punch, 20, 42, 70–4, 76, Figs. 2–4, 122, 150; safety, 142; snap punch, 20–1, 73, 76, Figs. 117, 121, 147; straight punches, 30, Fig. 17
punching pads, 30–1
punching posts, 15, 115
Pyongwon pattern, 84

range, 18; pre-arranged sparring, 88
ready stance, 24–5, Fig. 7
recoil, 17–18
referees, competitions, 107–8, 110
reverse crescent kick, 52, 79, Figs. 72–4, 128; flying reverse crescent kick, 57, Fig. 85
reverse knife hand, 34, Figs. 26, 27
reverse knife hand block, 61
reverse punch, 20, 42, 70–4, 76, Figs. 2–4, 122, 150
reverse turning kick, 39, 52–4, 74, 105, Fig. 75
running on the spot, 125

safety, 137–43; free sparring, 14, 102
Sam-il pattern, 84
scissors step, 44–5, 73–4; Fig. 145
scoring: competitions, 110–12; free sparring, 14
Se-jong pattern, 84
semi-forward stance, 25–6, 29
shadow fighting, 102
shin, as a weapon, 38
shin guards, 14, 107
side kick, 48, 105, Figs. 55–64, 138; flying side kick, 54, Figs. 78–80

side snap kick, 38
side thrust kick, 21–2, 38–9,
  Figs. 5, 36
single-step sparring, 13, 90–7
  Figs. 131–51
Sipjin pattern, 84
sit-ups, 126–7, Figs. 154, 155
skin, callouses, 114–15, 143
smoking, 138
snap punch, 20–1, 73, 76, Figs.
  117, 121, 147
So-san pattern, 84
Songmu Kwan, 8
sparring: free sparring, 88,
  98–105, 143; multi-step, 13;
  one-step, 13, 90–7, Figs.
  131–51; pair-form, 12, 13;
  pre-arranged, 72, 86–7, Figs.
  131–51; three-step, 89–90
spear hand, 118
speed training, 124–5
Sports Council, 140
stances, 23–9, Figs. 10–16;
  advancing stance, 27;
  attention stance, 24, Fig. 6;
  back stance, 26–7, 28, 29,
  Fig. 11; closed stance, 24;
  combination techniques, 71;
  crane stance, 27; fighting
  stance, 24, 29, Figs. 9, 116,
  120, 125; forward stance, 24,
  26, 29, Figs. 10, 14; free
  sparring, 102–3; hourglass
  stance, 28; natural stance,
  25; ready stance, 24–5, Fig.
  7; semi-forward stance,
  25–6, 29; straddle stance, 24,
  28, 29, Fig. 13; tiger stance,
  28–9, Fig. 12; walking stance,
  25, 29, Fig. 8; X-stance,
  27–8, 29
standing bow, 12, Fig. 1
static absorbtion, recoil, 17–18
stomach, high-energy punches,
  19–20
stone, destruction techniques,
  116
straddle stance, 24, 28, 29, Fig.
  13
straight punches, 30, Fig. 17
stretching exercises, 13, 123–4,
  130–5, 142, Figs. 161–70
strikes: destruction techniques,
  114; elbow strike, 18, 35–7,
  Figs. 29–33, 137; horizontal
  strike, 32; turning knee
  strike, 38
suppleness training, 123–35

Taebaek pattern, 84
taegueks, 84–5, 164–79
targets, destruction techniques,
  116–18

teachers, 10, 100–1, 113,
  139–40
tendons, 123
three-step sparring, 89–90
thrusting front kick, 44
tiger stance, 28–9, Fig. 12
tiles, destructions techniques,
  115–16, 118
timing, pre-arranged sparring,
  89
Toi-gye pattern, 85
Tong-il pattern, 85
training, 10–11, 12–15; free
  sparring, 101–3; patterns,
  81–5; safety, 142–3
training halls, safety, 141–2
turning kick, 22, 45–8, 59,
  70–1, 72, 74–6, 79, 104–5,
  Figs. 49–54, 115, 129–30,
  146, 151; flying turning kick,
  54, Figs. 76, 77; reverse
  turning kick, 39, 52–4, 105,
  Fig. 75
turning knee strike, 38
turns, 29, Figs. 14–16

Ul-ji pattern, 85
upright back fist, 31

vitamin supplements, 101

walking stance, 25, 29, Fig. 8
warming-up exercises, 13, 142
weapons, 30–9, Figs. 17–38
weight divisions, competitions,
  108–9
withdrawal, pre-arranged
  sparring, 88
women: competitions, 109;
  press-ups, 126; protective
  clothing, 107; training, 101
Won-hyo pattern, 85
wood, destruction techniques,
  115–17
World Taekwondo Federation
  (WTF), 9
wrist, blocking techniques, 61

X-block, 61, 62, 67, Figs. 86–9
X-stance, 27–8, 29

Yong-ge pattern, 85
Yoo-sin pattern, 85
Yul-kok pattern, 85